Quickest Way to Insanity –
Homeschool Your Kids

BY JULIE ANDERSON

3L Publishing
Sacramento, California

Library of Congress Control Number: 2009908010

ISBN-13: 978-0-578-03605-2

3L Publishing (www.3LPublishing.com) soft-cover edition September 2009.

Printed in the United States of America.

Cover Photo by Dale Kolke

Graphic Design by Erin Pace

Icon illustrations provided by iStockPhoto.com/
lushik, marko187, addan, 03519n

*To all families who are taking the wonderful
homeschooling journey together.
May this book assist you in your success!*

Table of Contents

Acknowledgments

First, thank you to 3L Publishing and their team for their tireless efforts in getting this project together — with a special shout out to Michelle (2L) for having such patience with me as a first-time author.

To Gina, thank you for your many hours of assistance and help with this book.

To my mom and sisters for understanding and supporting my *insanity* over the years.

A special thank you to my friend and mentor Arlene Taylor for teaching me so much about the brain and giving me her invaluable input for the book.

To my awesome daughter-in-law, Shawna for her help and support with the business. You are a wonderful addition to our family.

To my loving and supportive husband, who sacrificed so much of himself to support the boys and me over the years so I could remain home and take this journey with them. For his encouragement and understanding as I worked long hours to make this project come together — Pauliwogg, I LOVE YOU!

Then last but definitely not least, my three sons and travel companions, Alex, Kasey and Colton. You stuck with me through our journey's uphill climbs, blowouts and roadblocks so we could enjoy the beautiful views and downhill glides. My life is definitely enriched because of our travels and experiences. I would never change a thing! I love you boys with all my heart.

Foreword

I wrote this book for all of the *insane* parents like me who are considering or who have already begun the wonderful journey known as homeschooling. On this road, you will sometimes encounter potholes, forks with more than two options and uphill climbs. However, you will also have those wonderful downhill slides that make every tear, feeling of frustration or moment of uncertainty worth it.

I will share my personal, always interesting, most of the time enjoyable, sometimes stressful, occasionally tearful, but never ever boring 15-year journey. Sometimes we hit those potholes straight on with a jolt — okay fine! I may have hit them so hard we blew up a tire or two. However, as my journey continued I did learn how to maneuver around potholes and sometimes avoid them entirely. My experience hopefully will help you to dodge a few more obstacles than I did.

Over the years, I learned a few tricks, found some great resources, identified helpful strategies, and met great people that made this journey my best trip ever. I desire the tools contained in this book to help you start, continue and always enjoy your trip as you share this very special time in your child's life. As in real life, there are many different paths or itineraries you can take to reach the same destination. I will try to highlight the different scenery options — sometimes the old country road or sometimes the whole interstate. I wrote this book with the goal to help you fully enjoy your trip to *insanity* and like me never regret a single moment or sacrifice made along the way!

JULIE ANDERSON

Chapter One

Benefits of Homeschooling:
Is This Insane Trip Worth It?

> *1. Confusion 2. Class Position 3. Indifference 4. Emotional Dependency 5. Intellectual Dependency 6. Provisional Self-Esteem 7. One Can't Hide. It is the great triumph of compulsory, government monopoly mass-schooling that among even the best of my fellow teachers, and among even the best of my students' parents, only a small number can imagine a different way to do things.*
>
> JOHN TAYLOR GATTO

Okay, so maybe you have not decided if you want to take this journey yet, or, maybe some of you have started but second-guess yourself and feel uncertain if you want to continue. I wrote this chapter to address those uncertainties. I will list a few things to ponder. Some of your brains may have a different opinion, but hopefully by the end of this book, you will understand the reasons I feel the way I do. For now, let's look at the many benefits homeschooling can offer your children plus provide a valuable life experience for you — a trip if you will that will bring you untold adventures. Let's get started.

Control the Quality of Your Children's Education

Let me start by being diplomatic. Many schools have wonderful plans and programs, but the sad fact is they don't have the staff or funding to implement them in a way that will have the best results. Most of the public schools are overcrowded and understaffed so they simply can't reach the needs of all of the students. I recently did ASL interpreting for a deaf client in a 6th-grade classroom. The class had about 18 students, and of course, one teacher and no teacher's aide. The teacher seemed to be a caring person, but had a difficult time keeping the class focused for any length of time. That's not surprising. Not every student has the same rate of learning or the same learning preference. Another problem, which we will discuss in a later chapter, relates to the difference in the way the male and female brains process information. For these reasons many children just simply fall through the cracks in the educational system. If a child falls behind in the early stages of school, he or she, quite often, never catches up.

By homeschooling you can avoid this roadblock. You can adjust your teaching and curriculum to fit each individual child's needs — and this adjustment allows them to excel in their strengths and NOT fall behind in their weaknesses. What could be an unachievable peak to traverse in a public school now becomes a gentle climb with an incred-

Homeschooling "Travel" Checklist

- ✓ Adjust teaching and curriculum
- ✓ Teach child at his or her level
- ✓ Spend enough time on one subject
- ✓ Avoid wasting time when not necessary
- ✓ Improve safety and security
- ✓ Spend more time with your kids
- ✓ Greater flexibility
- ✓ Improve physical and emotional health

ible vista at the top, with a view that your child may never be able to see if not for being homeschooled.

You can teach your child at his or her own level. We all know some children start out learning slower than others, but if nurtured correctly children can "catch up" or level out as it were. Let's face it, just because you are 10-years-old it doesn't mean you will learn the same way or at the same pace as all other 10 year olds. Your child is an individual with a brain as unique as their thumbprint. So is the way they learn. If you force them to learn at the same pace and in the same way as everyone else, they simply wind up "memorizing" lessons only to pass them, quickly forgetting the information afterward. I don't know about you but I don't remember all of the United States presidents in order of service or the periodic table of elements. Do you? But I passed all the tests with flying colors in school. If I tried now to remember chemical compounds and formulas, I would probably blow up the house!

When you are homeschooling you can spend the time necessary on each subject with your child so that they "get it." You can find balance and avoid "over-doing" it so that your child doesn't become frustrated, thinking they are stupid or wrong. How sad that would be! Our kids have enough attacks on their self-esteem and there is no need to add this to it. You also don't have to spend unnecessary amounts of time going over information that your child fully understands already. Why take 45 minutes going over a subject that they get in 15? The extra time will only bore and irritate your child to the point where a subject he or she usually enjoys becomes one they can't stand anymore. In a classroom, this often results in smart kids getting in trouble for goofing off.

When you homeschool, you also have more control over what type of curriculum is used. In later chapters, I will discuss the different curriculum types available and how to understand your child's individual brain and how to choose the books and products that best fit each one.

Safety and Security

Students face many dangers in schools today. When my oldest was age 4, around the time that I was supposed to be enrolling him in kindergarten, the coach from the elementary school he would have been attending was arrested for molesting students. This problem has unfortunately become a common occurrence. Schools don't offer the same safety as your home. Concern for children's safety arises from unscrupulous people in positions of authority and from their peers.

Caring, concerned and aware parents want to protect children from drugs, alcohol and bullying. I don't personally think that we should make our children become "shut-ins." They need to fully understand the dangers that exist in real life. However, I also believe that they do not have to experience everything personally in order to learn how to be cautious judiciously and appropriately. By keeping our children safely at home we can educate them about the real world and protect them at the same time.

 **Travel Alert**

Your kids have a lifetime to spend without you — why lose their entire childhood spent in a classroom with four walls?

Spending More Time with Our Kids

Homeschooling also offers the wonderful benefit of simply time. Life today is incredibly fast-paced. Between work and responsibilities at home or in the community we have little time left. Then our kids are away so much. It's not only the six or seven hours at school, but also the time that they spend in travel to and from school. And don't forget about the homework! Nowadays children rarely come home from school with only an hour or so to spend on homework. Try three, or sometimes more! This time doesn't account for their involvement in after-school activities. It all adds up to a huge chunk of your child's life you miss. We only have them at home for 20 or so years. If your child is in public school, how many years of time do you actually lose? Let's figure it out. If you multiplied the hours in the day by the days in the school week by the weeks they are in school you would have … wait a minute! I am done with homeschooling! You figure it out. Anyway you get the point. You don't miss much of those awesome "I get it" or "Wow" moments when you have them at home with you, which (in my opinion) are the best parts of the journey. The memories you make here, the pictures forever imbedded in your mind of your child's face are, quite simply, priceless.

Greater Flexibility

What do I mean by this? Well, I have already mentioned flexibility in curriculum and pace, but also you literally have more options to how you spend each day. You can incorporate education whenever you travel. You can take the school books with you or simply teach them real lessons wherever you go. Imagine taking a road trip through Wyoming and Yellowstone. Why read about geysers and hot springs when you can go see them first hand? Or while taking a trip from Sacramento, California though the Altamont Pass you can watch the windmills as they generate alternate forms of energy. There is no better way to learn about the cycle of decomposition than to go for a hike while on a camping trip and investigate the old dead trees and see the teaming insect life they support or fauna fertilized from decaying matter. What better classroom than a forest? All this can be done on family trips. When you homeschool, you chose the schedule, curriculum and pace. How great is that?!

Physical and Emotional Health

We all know if you want to expose yourself to a hot house of germs, bacteria and icky parasites, go to school. We teach our children to share, but in the public school system, there are simply things we wish kids would keep to themselves. Just for the fun of it, I did a Google search with the keywords "sick schools" and it brought up 39,200,000 results. It listed everything from environmental hazards to the spread of the common cold. Sorry if it sounds like I am bashing public or even private schools. It is just a fact that if one child walks into a room with a cold or flu or, dare I say it, *lice*, it won't be long before his or her classmates get it. Some believe that this exposure builds your immunity later in life. I say, "Would you like a box of tissue?" We can build immunity just fine on our own thank you.

Then there is the much more important emotional health. I once heard a motivational speaker say that there is no greater assault on your self-esteem than the unkind words from significant people in your life. Teachers have a huge impact on our lives. I am sure we can all remember that one wonderful teacher that inspired us or made us laugh; but what about the ones that degraded us, making us feel stupid? The teachers who got angry when we did a lesson wrong or neglected to turn in our homework on time?

Referring back to the experience I had in the 6th-grade classroom, the teacher at one point was collecting an assignment that was supposed to have been completed. When she took it from one student, the girl informed her that she was not finished yet. The teacher simply said, "Too bad." In the opinion of the teacher, the student had been given plenty of time to complete the assignment. Well, it is true there had been an appropriate amount of time allowed, *if* that child understood the assignment. I had watched as the class busily worked on the project, but also noticed that a few of the students did not fully understand what was expected of them. Their questions were overlooked, and therefore, they were unable to complete the assignment. It wasn't their fault. Yet their self-esteem was hit because they "failed," as it were, to do what they were told — an emotional hit for sure. Another chapter in the book will discuss how closely connected the immune system and emotion are — and how if you are emotionally down you can literally get physically ill. Most of this can be avoided if we take advantage of the home-schooling opportunity.

I hope these benefits of homeschooling are enough to help you see this as a journey worth taking. And if you have already started this trip you may be experiencing some doubts. By keeping this information in mind, you can reinforce your determination to continue. So get packing, let's load the car, and fill up the gas tank. Your adventure is ready to begin!

Chapter Two

Explore the Options:
Which Roadmap Do I Choose?

An orchestra requires men with different talents and, within limits, different tastes; if all men insisted upon playing the trombone, orchestral music would be impossible. Social co-operation, in like manner, requires differences of taste and aptitude, which are less likely to exist if all children are exposed to the same influences than if parental differences are allowed to affect them.

BERTRAND RUSSELL

Okay, so you made your decision to take this exciting journey to insanity with your kids, now what? Do you just go buy some pencils and paper and start teaching? Of course not, like any seasoned traveler would, you need to prepare first. Find a roadmap, make a list of necessities, and of course, pack your bags. You will encounter several forks in the road where you have to choose which way to go. Think of your homeschooling options as a set of roadmaps.

Some "maps" have a lot of information on them, mileage charts, points of interest, lodging, etc. While other more basic "maps" require some research and time invested in finding out all of the necessary information. You will most importantly need to make your decision based on the best map for you and your family. Some choices will prove to be more laborious than others. With each of these options, I will present what I believe to be the pros versus cons — or should I say "downhill glides" versus "uphill climbs" of each road. So, let's take a look at basic options.

Complete Independence

Travel Alert

If you chose the map of "complete independence," check for state legal requirements.

When you choose to be completely independent of any established homeschooling program, you enjoy benefits such as independent decision making and no authority figure to answer to except your family. You don't have reports to fill out or teachers who hold you accountable. You can choose your own curriculum and schedule, and set up all your own field trips and vacations. You will only need to check into any legal requirements of your county or state. Some states require that you become your own school.

For example, in the state of California if this was the option that I had chosen, I would have become "Anderson's Homeschool" and been on file with California as an actual school. While this requirement may irritate some of you and make you frustrated that "Big Brother" looks over your shoulder, try to remember that these laws were established for the protection of our children. Remember that time in history called the "Industrial Revolution" where we moved off the farms and into the cities? During this time children — because of circumstances beyond their control — had to work to earn money for the family. This meant they were not receiving an education. So to counteract the problem the government established laws to protect them and see that each child got an education. While it may be a pain in the rear, following the filing requirements can save a lot of headaches in the future. Beyond this requirement you have a great deal of freedom to do what you want. So please check with your individual state to ensure you fulfill legal requirements before you start.[1]

 **Travel Alert**

Freedom to choose your own curriculum also means you are responsible for the choice.

Now, this choice comes with some daunting terrain. First, your independence may lead to feelings of isolation. You may encounter challenges with school subjects, frustration as you get your kids to do their work, or inability to find certain resources and aid. Freedom to choose your own curriculum also means you have the *responsibility* to choose it. Sorting though a large variety of books and material can become quite confusing. In addition, the costs can also add up quickly with this option. Books are not cheap. When you also have more than one child each with a different learning style, it can get even more costly. Then depending on where you live, interaction with other children may be limited. This means that you as a parent will have to be more creative to address these issues.

One more thing, recognition as an accredited school matters to some parents. Lack of accreditation means that some colleges may not recognize your children's schooling — and thus, make it difficult to enroll. They may require additional testing for acceptance. However, with the huge variety of college options this may or may not matter to you — but for some it may prove to be an issue.

[1] Two websites I have found to be helpful are www.schoolandstate.org and www.netstate.com. These have a lot of information on the requirements of many states.

Travel Alert

Try not to allow the seemingly "high mountains" to prevent you from making the trek. All obstacles can be overcome.

Try not to allow these seemingly high mountains make you not choose to homeschool. Many ways exist to cope with each "climb." The feeling of isolation can be overcome by joining local support groups. We also have the wonderful thing known as the Internet. While I personally believe information overload exists on the Net, cyberspace can prove to be an invaluable aid for homeschooling families that may not live near support groups. Many homeschooling chat groups attract other parents who can lend support and supply you with that "spare tire" if you have a homeschooling "blow out" or give you a gallon or two of gas if you run low (unless you're taking your homeschooling journey in a hybrid). I have no doubt that you will find someone who has come across the same problem you experience and can provide assistance. As far as the interaction with other kids, join a community-based youth program or involve the whole family in volunteer activities in your area. Put your kids in gymnastics or have them join a local drama or music group. Don't overlook volunteering to work with the elderly. You can never put a price tag on the wisdom and experience they can share with your kids.

Independent Study Programs

Your local public school supports or controls independent study programs. Those programs close to home can be very convenient. Your student normally has an appointment once a week with a teacher at the local school. The teacher corrects the previous week's work and gives out the next week's assignments. Since local public schools run these programs, they don't have costs associated with them. You have paid for it through your tax dollars. Your child can use the library and computer lab at the school. Most of these schools

Travel Alert

Independent Study Programs offer a very good option for "split-decision" parents.

allow for the child to have access to everything that the students enrolled in the school have — including sports, music programs, shop programs, field trips, etc. These programs offer a very good option for what I like to call "split-decision" parents.

For example, I had a good friend who wanted to homeschool her children but her husband wanted them in public school because he wanted them involved in football. This option would satisfy both parents' desires.

The lack of flexibility and control often makes this option the biggest "uphill climb" or drawback. You have no choice over the curriculum or schedule. The books you get are the books you get. You have set grade-level expectations. You have little to no flexibility to make your schedule. Some schools may require that you keep a log of time spent on each subject. My sister used this option for awhile for her son. She had to fill out a time card for each day and record 45 minutes spent on each subject every day. This was required whether or not practice was needed in every subject.

If your child is not vaccinated, this option can also prove to be problematic. Your child technically attends a public school and interacts with other children so pressure to vaccinate exists the same as required for public-school students.

Stigma can also be another "uphill climb" with this option. One of the reasons this type of program was originally developed was to provide schooling for pregnant teens or "problem students." I have to go on record as saying that I take offense to the term "problem student." In my years of study on the brain, it is apparent that children labeled with this negative pejorative are most often "extreme introverts" or "extreme extroverts." (A discussion of these two terms will be considered in a later chapter). Maybe they just have a learning style not adequately addressed in the classroom. For these reasons, they may withdraw and be seen as "not a team player" or ask a lot of questions and labeled a "trouble maker." Whatever the case, independent-study programs may have this reputation attached to them so you might need to develop a strong backbone to deal with looks or unsolicited comments.

Proficiency testing creates the final drawback of this choice. Testing ... yuck! Don't even get me started! Enrollment in public school requires you have your child take these silly, little fill-in-the-bubble tests. Yes, in order to take advantage of this option, testing becomes a necessary evil and I do mean *EVIL*.

Private Homeschools

Private homeschools include two basic types: online correspondence schools and small private local community homeschooling programs. The "downhill slides" or pros provide organized work done for you. You pay a fee and they supply books and often assignments. You mail or deliver completed work to them; and they grade it and supply you with the next set of assignments. You have a support system with this option that varies in amount and quality dependant on the one that you choose. Some schools are accredited, which makes it easier to enter into a college program if your child wants that in the future. So for many parents this option creates more "downhill coasting" than "uphill climbs."

In my opinion, this option creates two (very steep) "climbs." First, you have little to no choice in curriculum. As with the previous option, the school pretty much decides what books to use, what schedule to keep and how much work to turn in. Second, cost is a consideration. Some of the programs can be costly and require an investment of thousands of dollars per child per year. This expense may mean you can't afford to use this "map."

Charter Schools

This choice can be a little confusing. Why? A wide variety of charter-school programs exist in the United States, which makes it difficult to make a choice. You may wonder, what is a charter school? The public funds elementary and secondary school via our tax dollars, but have been freed from some of the rules, regulations and statutes that apply to other public schools. In exchange for this freedom, charter schools must provide some type of accountability and produce certain results, which are noted in each school's charter. Not all charter schools are homeschools or offer homeschooling options. For example, here in the town where I live, there is a charter school of the arts and another one that uses the Montessori method of teaching — but many do offer homeschooling or have been set up specifically to support the homeschooling community. You may also find a charter that supports homeschooling but limits your choices as a parent. So, if you select this option you have to do your homework (pardon the pun).

Travel Tip

The charter school "roadmap" selection has pros and cons — it contains many narrow alleys or spacious-wide roads.

If you choose this "roadmap," it will show many narrow alleys or spacious-wide roads. Some charter programs give you as much freedom of choice as the "complete independence route" or as limited as the public independent-study programs. Whatever the guidelines of a particular charter school, most schools will provide some level of financial support. Remember, they are considered a public school so tax dollars support them. These funds can be used for qualifying field trips, books or curriculum, and basic school supplies (i.e., pens, paper, and ink for printers, etc.). If you do your research and find the right one you can choose whatever books you want — and they will be purchased for you with the allotted funds.

The "uphill climbs" with this option include doing your research to find the ones that best fit you and your family; and understand that charter schools demand some of the same requirements as public school enrollment, which means that you agree to do the pesky bubble tests and supply them with samples of your child's work. The freedom of choice makes this option a worthwhile selection. In my opinion, if you choose this "map" you have to insist on being supplied with the curriculum that best fits the brain of each of your children (see chapters three, four and seven for more information).

This is the "map" that I chose. Over 15 years that I homeschooled, I used three different charters. I left the first two, which in the beginning offered flexibility of choice and funding to support my choices. However, after a couple of years they changed their policies. As a result, I changed my choice. I simply went back to my "roadmap" and decided on a different direction. In the end, we still made it to our desired destination. A very important point I will emphasize throughout this book: If one program or "map" doesn't work for you or your children, simply change to one that fits your family better. Even within the option you can insist on more choices. Remember, you are in control; you are the teacher; and these are your kids. No one knows better than you what is best for them. Don't allow anyone to sell you a "map" you don't want or one that will not work for you and your family. It's YOUR choice!

Travel Tip

Meditation time gives you peace of mind to consider your options and different "maps."

So, now comes some serious meditation time for you to consider your options. Consider the different "maps" I have described and how each one fits your family. However, wait a bit before you make your decision. There is more to consider and further preparation and "packing" to do. Your success or failure depends on good preparation. Knowing what to pack and then making sure you have it all with you can also affect the amount of enjoyment you will have on this trip. Let's move on and discuss some of the things you need to think about when packing for your journey.

Chapter Three

Let's Start Packing, But What?

> ❝ *Shaped a little like a loaf of French country bread, our brain is a crowded chemistry lab, bustling with nonstop neural conversations.* ❞
>
> DIANE ACKERMAN

Now that you understand the different "maps" or support systems to choose from, you have to move onto "packing." Each child has specific needs, and these needs should be addressed in the homeschooling situation to ensure that he or she — and you as a parent — have a successful and productive experience. For example, if you have a child with special diet needs or medications you would make sure that in preparation for a trip or vacation, you packed everything needed to care for him or her, right? Failure to pack correctly could potentially lead to a disaster — one that could cause you to cut your trip short. When it comes to homeschooling, parents who do not start out prepared and ready for the experience might decide to go back to traditional education. If you cut your homeschooling "trip" off early you could miss countless awesome experiences.

One of our "family stories" illustrates this very well. Our friends recently hosted a music weekend on their 20-acre property in the country. Most of us just drove out each day, but my son and some of his friends (including a buddy named Alec) asked if they could camp out for the weekend. A great group of our friends and associates were also staying — and for this reason my husband and I gave him permission. He promptly went home to pack- to gather the necessary things.

When I arrived at our friend's house the next morning, I asked "Well, son, how did you sleep?"
"Horrible!" was his reply.
I then asked: "You forgot a mat and had to sleep on the ground, didn't you?"
"Yes," he admitted. "And I was quite cold too. Alec and I slept in the cab of my truck."

Okay, you have to understand the hilarity in this situation. My son is 6'2" with most of that height in his legs. The truck he was referring to is a *little* Nissan pickup. After further questioning, it turned out that when my son went home to get the things necessary to spend the night what he actually packed was a tent. No sleeping bag, no cushions, and no blankets — not even a pillow! When I asked if he was going to stay the night again he replied, not surprisingly, "No." This little family story has application because my son missed out on a second night of fun, why? He was not prepared well enough for the first night.

Travel Tip

As you "pack" don't forget to bring your "brain."

So as you "pack" for your homeschooling journey, you have to consider the brain of each child. Each person's brain is as unique as their fingerprints. Each person has strengths and weaknesses. Each child's brain has a preferred way to best receive and process information.

Most people are aware there are three basic learning or sensory styles. These are visual (a.k.a., visuals), auditory (a.k.a., auditories) and kinesthetic, (a.k.a., kinesthetics). The importance of this is huge. Each person, adult or child, has a tendency to learn better in one of the three styles. Determining the learning style of your child affects what curriculum you choose for each child you teach. I cannot emphasize this next point enough. As we discuss these different styles we will highlight their differences. You must, however, always remember: *Different means UNLIKE — not superior or inferior — just different.*

It is tough to figure out a young child's innate brain preferences. In a few children, however, it can be more obvious. With my youngest son, Colton, it was apparent fairly early in his life that he was a kinesthetic learner. Early on my second son, Kasey, appeared to be a kinesthetic, but by the time he was 11 or 12 years old, we began to realize that he was truly an auditory learner. Life as an infant was very difficult for Kasey so he had a lot of kinesthetic input. This stimulation may have led him to develop this as part of his brain quite strong since it was reflected in his personality. However, in time his natural learning preference became obvious (he is an auditory). After you grasp a clear understanding of each learning style you can try to identify your own.[2] Then watch for signs or clues that help you to best guess each child's preferences.

Visual Learners

I begin with this learning preference since most experts agree that approximately 60 percent of the population are visual learners. My own findings lean more toward 50 percent, but either way the majority of children and adults will have this particular preference. You can pay attention to things in someone's personality that can give you a clue as to his or her preference. Listed below are some of the personality characteristics that you will see in the visual learners.

[2] To help you in determining your sensory/learning preference, go to www.quickestwaytoinsanity.com to download a worksheet.

Visual brains obviously process information most efficiently and effectively based on what they take in through their eyes. Sometimes if you pay attention to the conversation you may hear it reflected in what they say. The visuals may say things like, "Do you *see* what I mean?" or "That *looks* good to me." Statements that use words connected to *sight*. They may always choose a "room with a view" over a quiet or comfortable one. Meanwhile, the other 40 to 50 percent of the population really don't care.

Travel Trivia

Visual learners:

Account for 50 to 60 percent of the population.

People with visual learning or communication styles often look well put together. Their clothes are always just-so and well-coordinated. No stains or mismatches. No plaids with strips and so on. The way things look is very important to them. They may purchase furniture based on the appearance even if it is uncomfortable. For example, I had a friend growing up whose mom ran a day care from her house. You would never know it. When you walked in the front room, the living area was immaculate. The furniture looked brand new. The whole thing looked like it was a showroom. When I asked my friend if they had just bought the couches, she replied, "No." It turned out that they just never used that room because her mom always wanted it to *look* right.

Visual Learning Styles

✓ Well-coordinated clothing

✓ Make purchases based on appearance

✓ Perfect-looking pets

✓ Visual career choices, such as photographer, sharpshooter or decorator

It was okay she said because the couches really weren't all that comfortable anyway. Her mom was definitely a visual.

You may also see a visual person with those perfect-looking pets. Maybe it's the poodle that goes to the groomer every week or the beautiful bird that might drive an auditory crazy, but they sure *look* good. They will pick up visual cues faster than the non-visuals. For example, if you have a piece of lint on your clothes or a hair out of place, they will notice.

Job choices sometimes can indicate whether a person is a visual or not. They will tend to choose careers where they can use their visual skills. You may find them in careers such as interior decorators, sharpshooters, photographers, window display coordinators for department stores or they may be artists. I have a good friend that is definitely a visual. She decorates million dollar homes — and she is insanely good at it. I once told her that I wanted to rearrange my living room, but I couldn't figure out what would look good. She took about 20 minutes, moved things around, opened up the view, and made it look completely different and a lot better.

As I said before, most of these traits are much easier to see in adults. However, if you watch closely you can see some tendencies in children. Visual children may be those that changes clothes three times a day because if they get the slightest little thing on them they want clean ones. Maybe they always choose the "pretty" toys or neatly line up their collection of toy cars. The visual child wants their pets to *look* pretty also. Perhaps putting ribbons on them or always brushing their pet's hair so they look good. They may not want food on their plates to touch because it doesn't look right. Perhaps, they may notice little visual things that other children don't. For example, hidden objects in story pictures or small pieces of lint on your clothing. If your child fits these descriptions he or she may be visual.

Visual Child Characteristics

✓ Frequently changes clothes

✓ Attracted to "pretty" toys

✓ Lines up toys in neat rows

✓ Avoids allowing food to *run together* looks wrong

Now the most important thing to remember — from relation-ships to communication to learning — *what visual learn-ers "take in through their eyes" usually will have a much bigger impact on them than anything else.* You can tell a visual you love them and you can give lots of hugs, but if you don't *show* it to them they may not "get it." In teaching, you can tell visual learners how it works or what to do, but for them to understand they must be shown through illustrations, graphics, diagrams, pictures and more.

My oldest child Alex has a visual brain. When he was younger he was very into (and still is, I might add) mechanics. I remember one day he came to me with an invention. He had created an alternative track system for cars ("So there will be less accidents, mom"). He explained his wonderfully imagi-native idea to me by drawing all of the intricate details on paper so I could understand them. To this day, when he is explaining mechanical information, he draws it out. So you can understand why I couldn't pack just any general textbooks for his "trip." I had to choose books that contained a lot of pictures, diagrams and illustrations.

Unfortunately, many public schools fail to account for different learning pref-erences. For example, a popular series of math books that many schools use has almost no pictures. The pages are sterile, black and white and contain no color. They include few charts or graphs — and the ones they do feature can only be found in the section on *charts and graphs*. How sad is that? This means that roughly 80 percent (60 visual and 20 kinesthetic) of the kids don't get it! What a waste of money, time and brain energy.

What do you "pack" for your little visuals? Books with a lot of pictures. Items to make the "school-work" area visually appealing. Put beautifully colored maps on the wall. Try using posters that have illustrations and pictures in them for the different subjects. For high school earth science, I used a visually appealing computer program. The student walked into a science building and could choose to enter into a library, science lab or resource room. It was interactive with lots of graphics — perfect for all three learning styles. You can even ask your visual child for his or her input on what books appeal to them. If your child chooses the one they like, chances are they will enjoy doing the work. Let them turn in paper work that reflects their visual styles. Maybe you get a lot of papers with mostly drawings. Who cares? Did they get the point? Did they learn the concept? Okay then you achieved success — and that is all that matters.

Travel Tip

✓ Visually appealing school work area

✓ Use posters and pictures

✓ Use computer programs with graphics

✓ Read books with lots of illustrations

Now let's move on to the next 20 percent of the population, auditory learners or "auditories."

Auditory Learners

Auditory learners process information most efficiently and effectively by what they hear or by what they read.[3] Since most of the teaching in public school classrooms comes in the form of spoken word or written instructions, this group of children generally

[3] This is because decoding of speech sounds and decoding of written signs-letters, words and numbers-happen in the same portion of the brain.

has a much easier time grasping ideas in school. Understand that I am not saying they will excel in all subjects. Other factors also come into play. Auditory learners generally tend to understand information and instruction delivered through lecture and written form, because they pick up and process information best through their ears. Their strengths come through listening and reading. You may notice in their conversations they use terms that refer to hearing. Perhaps phrases like, "That *sounds* right to me," or, "I *hear* what you are saying." If you know someone like this they may be an auditory.

The way that things sound is very important to them. I am an auditory learner and let me tell you this is so true. We feel easily irritated by sounds that

Auditory Learning Styles

✓ Sound is important

✓ Easily irritated by noise

✓ Pet selection by how they sound

✓ Choose careers as counselors, musicians or entertainers

most people don't even notice. Let me share a story. For example, one night my husband had just turned out the light and gotten into bed. As we lay there trying to fall asleep, I tuned into a slight tapping sound. My husband insisted that I was hearing things (well, I was!). I got out of bed and turned on the light three times, trying to locate the source of the noise because it was driving me crazy. Finally, I followed my ears into the bathroom where a small flying bug kept hitting the mirror! Sadly the little guy met an untimely yet speedy end and I was able to finally get a good night's sleep.

Like visuals, auditories can also be picky about clothes, furniture or their pets. They may choose pets and clothing based on how they sound or don't

Auditory Child Characteristics

✓ Avoids fabrics that make noise

✓ Attracted or repelled by toys that make noise

✓ Attracted or repelled by pets that do or do not make certain noise

sound. Yes, clothes do make sounds. I remember back in the late 70's corduroy pants were all the rage. Like most teenagers, I wanted to fit in with the rest, but I drew the line at corduroy pants. They were so *noisy* — and don't get me started on taffeta! I am drawn to certain animals connected to their sounds. For example, small dogs like Pomeranians are adorable (to look at), but I would never own one — I don't like their "yappy" barks. Turtles too, yes turtles. My sons had a box turtle named Michael Angelo. I could not be in the room while he ate his lettuce. He made a terribly annoying "crunchy" noise.

Personal preference matters too. An irritating sound to one auditory may be pleasant for another. Sounds — whether auditory learners consider them good or bad — are important to them.

Auditories often gravitate toward jobs or careers as counselors, musicians, radio or television entertainers or hosts, translators, writers or public speakers — essentially any career field that allows them to talk or listen to people talk.

Travel Trivia

Auditory learners:

Account for about 20 percent of the population.

They tend to pick up on auditory cues faster than visual or kinesthetic stimuli. They may notice a slight change in the tone of a person's voice. Small irregular sounds in a car engine that no one else notices can become very obvious to an auditory. Someone jangling keys in their pocket can be unbearable for an auditory but not even be heard by visuals or kinesthetic learners.

Travel Tips

✓ How you "say" it counts

✓ Focus on reading materials (e.g., books and magazines)

✓ Provide writing tools

✓ Vocalize positive reinforcement

✓ Be careful to keep environment quiet when appropriate

With the auditory child, you may find that they talk to themselves a lot. Confession time, auditory adults do that too. You may walk past their room to hear them engrossed in a deep conversation only to peer inside to find they are talking to a toy. In my case, it was an imaginary friend named Maynard. Auditory children love to read everything. They might read road signs or labels just to hear the sound of a voice. These little ones can be more sensitive or frightened by sounds. They may be the ones that can't sleep during a thunder storm or complain about the wind blowing the tree limbs against the window. If you recognize some of these traits in your children, they may be an auditory.

You may recall me saying that my second son, Kasey is an auditory? This learning style became clear when around age 11 to 12 years old he began devouring books like they were chocolate. We would go to the bookstore to buy a few books, and then before I knew it, he had finished reading them all and was asking for more. He now has a collection of hundreds of books ranging from biblical topics to science fiction. Some of them he has even read two or three times. When Kasey had alone time I would often find him reading something, anything, it didn't really matter. This even got him in trouble a time or two. For example, sometimes I noticed a light coming from his room around 20 to 30 minutes after bedtime. What would I find? He was reading a science fiction book or magazine under the covers, which is typical for an auditory child.

In building your relationship with an auditory learner, you must remember *how you "say" it.* Hearing the words "good job" or saying "I love you" is so much more important than a pat on the back or a hug. Be especially careful of harsh words or silent treatments with this group. They feel great sensitivity to voice tones. Their brains register auditory messages faster and with more emotion than the other two preferences. The lesson learned? Little auditory ones need plenty of verbal reassurance.

So what do you "pack" for your auditory children? I would say plenty of reading material, books, magazines, etc. Be sure to also include a variety of writing utensils so they can write down all their wonderful thoughts. You don't have to be generally choosy about your academic books — even the books with lots of pictures and graphics always have plenty of words. Music CDs and books on tape work well for this group. You may also want to pick a noise-free "vehicle" for this trip that lacks annoying sounds. When "auditories" concentrate on a particular subject, a quiet environment might be really important for them.

Okay, two sensory preferences down one to go. I discuss this one last because, in my opinion, we need to validate this group the most. You will have to get creative on what you "pack" for them — especially for teenagers. Let's continue and I will explain why.

Kinesthetic Learners

Approximately 20 to 30 percent of the population are kinesthetic learners. Most experts in this field say that the figure is closer to 20 percent — and let me say I am by no means what I consider an "expert"; however, I kept

Travel Trivia

Kinesthetic learners make up about 20 to 30 percent of the population.

my own private records. If I add up the results from all of the workshops and classes that I have held on this subject my findings are different. The figures consistently come out at approximately 30 percent kinesthetic and only 50 percent visual. The auditory preference seems to remain at 20 percent. Most male attendees have turned out to be kinesthetic. No matter whose figures are correct, we know that at least a portion of our children do have this learning style preferred in their brains. Let's take a look at the characteristics you may find prevalent in kinesthetic learners. Then picture yourself and those you know to see whether or not you have a few in your close relationships.

What exactly is a kinesthetic learner? It is the portion of the population that processes information most efficiently and effectively by touch, taste and smell. Some consider these people to be "touchy-feely." They may also have a strong "gut" sense. For this reason in conversations you may find them

Kinesthetic Learning Styles

✓ Comfort counts

✓ Purchases made on how they feel

✓ Pets chosen based on touch

✓ Career choices like craftsperson, painter or dancer

using terms that reflect this feeling such as, "This doesn't feel right," or, "My gut is telling me something is wrong." They are usually right. My husband is a powerful kinesthetic. He uses these terms all the time and most of the time his *bad feeling* about a specific situation turns out to be correct.

Kinesthetic Child Characteristics

✓ Picky about food textures

✓ Show sensitivity about their personal space

✓ Comfortable clothes are a must

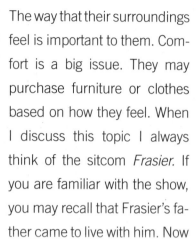

The way that their surroundings feel is important to them. Comfort is a big issue. They may purchase furniture or clothes based on how they feel. When I discuss this topic I always think of the sitcom *Frasier*. If you are familiar with the show, you may recall that Frasier's father came to live with him. Now the character Frasier was obviously a visual. His furnishings always reflected a clean, neat style. I think his father must have been a kinesthetic. Why do I say this? Remember the chair that his father brought with him? You know the one that was smack in the middle of the living room? It was an old, well-used recliner that had clearly gone out of style. It did not fit the living room décor. It remained because it provided his father necessary comfort. To his credit, Frasier did not throw out the old chair. Now I know it was only a TV show, but what a wonderful example of a visual who validated a kinesthetic's needs.

Typically, for kinesthetic brains appearance will almost always take second place to comfort. For this reason, they may choose pets that appeal to touch. They may bring home that not-so-attractive dog from the pound — one that scares away the visual or has an unpleasant bark that annoys the auditory. The kinesthetic however, feels differently about the pup that jumps on his or her lap and cuddles — the way it looks doesn't matter.

You may also find they lean toward careers that make good use of their natural abilities. Hands-on jobs like woodworkers, artists, potters, painters, dancers, athletes, counselors or surgeons.[4] I remember my aunt, a registered nurse,

---

[4] They are good in this field because they *sense* things or have that *gut* feeling. Not to be confused with the auditory brain who are good counselors because they like to talk and are good at listening.

Travel Tip

✓ Positive reinforcement through physical affection

✓ Avoid physical confrontation

✓ Provide activities that involve touch (e.g., finger painting, Play-Doh™)

✓ Allow comfortable attire

✓ Perform hands-on learning exercises

telling me years ago how people who want to work in the surgical field have to learn to tie a knot with surgical string with two fingers. Wow! I have tried it. It's not that easy. I can't do it. Of course, I'm not a kinesthetic either.

For children in this learning-style group, you may find they're picky about food textures. They may always have the family dog or cat sit with them. They tend to sit or stand close to or lean on their parents or whoever they feel comfortable around. They often show sensitivity about their personal space around strangers and around individuals who they do not trust. Comfortable clothes are a must. Have you ever had a young child cry when you try to put certain clothes on them? Only to have them quickly remove them as soon as they get the chance. Perhaps they insist on the same old and stained set of clothes. If this sounds familiar, your child is likely kinesthetic. Physical confrontation can also be emotionally devastating for them. While a slap on the hand of a visual or auditory may pass without hardly any reaction, a kinesthetic may be deeply affected.

We must remember something extremely important about the kinesthetic in our life. *What they 'feel' in their relationships is of incredible importance.* The need to give them proper physical reassurance in the form of hugs, hand holding, or rubs on the shoulders cannot be overemphasized. This physical comfort can be extremely difficult in our society. Improper and proper touch can sometimes be difficult to separate. So let them set the guidelines. Follow their lead about their comfort level when it comes to physical connections.

I am blessed to have two wonderful kinesthetics in my immediate family — my husband and youngest son, Colton. Words cannot express what a difference this knowledge has made in my marriage. For years, I could not understand why my husband would get grumpy when I didn't sit right next to him on the couch or hold his hand when we were together. When this would happen, I would inquire why it so deeply affected him. He would always respond that it *felt* (kinesthetic) like I didn't love him. What? Remember, I am auditory. I *told* him all the time that I loved him — and there was the problem. I told him when what I needed to do was make sure that he *felt* that I loved him. It may sound like a small thing, but it had a huge impact on our relationship. When I made those small adjustments and started communicating with him on *his* brain's preference, what a difference it made in our relationship. What a positive difference!

Now for Colton, well where do I start? As I mentioned earlier from a very young age it became apparent that he was a kinesthetic. For example, I would tell him to go put something clean and nice on so we could go to the store. What would he do? He would simply change from one comfortable old and stained set of clothes to another. He was constantly petting, holding or cuddling our animals. I don't think that a day ever passed in his life before the age of 10 that you could not find him at some point sitting on the floor or couch rubbing his finger through their fur. To this day at 176 lbs and 6'2," he will still try to sit on my lap. Since that doesn't work so well anymore, he just sits really close to me often with his head resting on my shoulder. These characteristics are typical of a kinesthetic learner — and to deny them physical contact and validation would be devastating.

Imagine how difficult it is for this group to survive in the typical school setting. First, the curriculum generally comes in an auditory format and is supported by pictures and graphs. What about the kinesthetic sense? Sure in the early primary grades K-3, you will find a lot of finger painting, Play-Doh™ and objects that can be manipulated to help you learn; but just because he or she moves on to junior high and high school, it doesn't automatically mean that your child doesn't need those "tactile" experiences anymore.

Consider the non-existent comfort in the average classroom. Hard tile or linoleum floors, drafty windows, and heat during the summer and cold during the winter. What about the chairs and desks? Hard wood or plastic, linked together so space and distance between chair and desk cannot be altered. Lined up in rows and often too close to each other. What were people thinking when they created those? Adults that work in offices, by law, have to be provided with ergonomically correct chairs and desks. Yet our poor little kids have to spend six or more hours a day and up to 12 years in these conditions. Then we expect them to learn and retain information while seated in uncomfortable furniture and learning in miserable surroundings. Yeah, I don't think so.

So what to "pack" for your little kinesthetics? First, very comfortable clothes and practice what I call "shoeless learning" this means allow them to wear slippers and be comfortable. Studies show that an uncomfortable feeling can interfere with the brain's ability to learn.

I know some homeschooling parents that insist on following the same model as regular schools. Their routine includes a structured environment where they insist their children get up, change out of their comfortable clothes, sit at a wood desk, and do school work. Might as well just send them off to school! A lack of orthodox structure offers one of the greatest benefits of homeschooling. Let them be comfortable. They don't even have to sit at a desk or table to learn. Most of the reading my kids did was on the couch in their sweats. Sometimes outside on the deck in one of those comfortable deck chairs or perhaps even stretched out on their beds. Some kids may learn best when they are up and moving, pacing around the room as they read. Remember the goal — to learn and retain information. It doesn't matter what physical position they learn in so long as they "get it."

When it comes to curriculum, "pack" some coins, jelly beans and cooking products. Yes, you did read it right. Provide "tools" or anything they can get their hands in to touch and feel. In Colton's case, most of his basic math skills came from counting and dividing edibles like jelly beans. Fun to handle plus you can eat them when you finish. Cooking also offers kinesthetics a wonderful way to learn. You will want to "pack" some tools for your trip too. Maybe shovels, rakes or tape measures. I will expand on how to use these in Chapter 6: Load Up! Let's Go, Getting Started. Trust me, kinesthetics will learn more from using these things than reading a textbook.

So there you have the main learning styles of the brain. Since we have discussed some information related to touch, I thought this would also be a good chapter to include some interesting statistics on the importance of touch. I also want to raise your awareness about the weakness of western culture when it comes to the importance of proper physical contact.

The Importance of Touch

It is interesting how U.S. culture views touch. We have a society concerned about the line between proper and improper touch. As a result, we often go overboard in avoiding it. For example, studies were conducted in coffee houses in France and the U.S. It was found that in France casual touch occurred some 200 times within a 30-minute time period. Yet in the U.S., casual touch only occurred twice in 30 minutes. What a contrast! In some nations, it is proper to give a hug as a greeting or send off; but here in the U.S., you will rarely ever go beyond a professional handshake.

What are the results? Well they are quite significant. Cross-cultural studies show that in societies where parents outwardly show more physical affection toward their children, there is a significantly lower rate of adult violence. What a message that sends! Another study was conducted in an eating-disorder clinic in California. They found that 85 percent of the participants were touch-deprived or touch-wounded kinesthetics. Please don't think that I am implying that 85 percent of all those with eating disorders are touch-deprived. This may have been one study, but 85% is a high number — and one that should make us think.

Studies conducted at the Touch Research Institute located at the University of Miami in Florida also yielded some interesting results. One famous study was done on touch and premature babies. A group of babies that were born premature were massaged for 15 minutes three times a day for 10 days. The group that received the massages gained 47 percent more weight than the non-massaged infants. They were also released from the hospital on the average of one week earlier than the non-massaged group. Again, some pretty significant findings.

There have been way too many studies on this subject to list. It does help us to appreciate how sensitive the different brains are to different sensory stimuli. You now hopefully have a better understanding of the main ways that our brains process information. I have no doubt if you apply this to your teaching methods you will notice very positive results.

Now let's move onto another facet of the brain that we need to consider. Introversion versus extroversion — that is, how much stimulus does my child's brain need?

Introversion versus Extroversion

Many people don't clearly understand this topic. All too often introverts are mistaken as shy. While people think that the extroverts are always outspoken. Well, this situation is not the case either. Some very introverted people are also the most outspoken and definitely not shy. In contrast, many extroverts would never dream of emphatically expressing their opinions.

Experts such as Katherine Benziger feel that 15 percent of the population sits at either end of the scale and the other 70 percent falls somewhere in between. This "middle" area is known as "ambiversion" — some individuals fall in the middle of ambiversion (e.g., require stimulation about half the time and relief from stimulation about half the time). Other individuals tend to lean toward the introverted or extroverted side. These terms refer to the amount of stimulation your brain requires in order to function optimally.

Sometimes you can begin to see tendencies to one side versus the other in babies. Introverted babies may be those that don't like to be held a lot. They are just happier at home in a quiet surrounding. They may cry and protest every time you get in the car and leave. Noisy surroundings make them fussy. On the other hand, little extroverted babies may take shorter naps. They may want to be held or amused all the time. They are happier in busier environments. It is important to understand this when planning to educate your children. You want their brains to be alert, happy and full of energy to maximize their learning ability.

To help you understand the difference between the extremes, let me use the analogy of our daytime awake hours. With the extreme in-

Travel Tip

Introverts prefer a low-stimulus environment — allow them to do their school work alone.

trovert it is like their brain is naturally self-stimulated. If they are awake for say 14 hours a day, 12 to 14 of those hours can be spent happily alone. They don't require a lot going on around them to be happy. As a matter of fact, too much external stimulus can overload their brains. For this reason they may limit their interactions with other people or avoid places with a lot of stimulus.

Introverts tend to steer away from high-risk situations, which can have the potential for too much stimulus. A low-stimulus environment is much better for them. Introverted children may prefer to work in quiet surroundings. They may choose to do their school work alone in their rooms. Allow them this flexibility. Their brains will likely function more energy efficiently.

Introverts tend to steer away from competition — unless it is a low stimulus competition like chess. These are the people or children that prefer to watch the game rather than participate. For example, my mom, four sisters, two nieces and I often get together to play games. Oh my word! What a loud group we become. For years one of my sisters would only play one or two games then quit. She would go over to a corner and quietly watch. The rest of us would roll our eyes and call her a party pooper and then continue with our out-of-control, loud games. How horrible I felt when I began my training in brain function and personality. It quickly hit me, my sister is an introvert stuck amongst a bunch of extroverts! We now fully understand when her brain hits its maximum stimulation. When she goes and sits somewhere else, we quiet down — well, we try to quiet down a little — and then allow her the space she needs. Above all we never take it personally!

Imagine how our introverts feel in public schools. For example, a noisy classroom with 20-plus students offers way too much stimulation for the typical introvert. So what happens? They quietly sit by themselves in the back of the class. Then they hope and pray that the teacher never calls on them.

This may be the reason they are often picked on and labeled "stuck up" or "loner." The teacher may even express concern during parent-teacher conferences that the student isn't a team player or perhaps is uncooperative in class. And those tests! The introverted portion of the population finds tests extremely painful. How sad for our little introverts. For these reasons, they are at higher risk for isolation and depression.

You may have a little introvert in your life — a child who enjoys reading quietly even if they aren't an auditory. Or maybe they spend a lot of time playing alone even when they can play with other children. If this is the case, be patient. Make the learning area quiet and non-threatening. Validate their need for a low-stimulus environment. Don't get me wrong, I especially believe homeschooled children need to socialize. No matter what career or life path they choose, they will need to learn to comfortably interact with other people. Just remember the hours in the day analogy. Keep the high-stimulus interactive times in balance throughout the week. Spread the extracurricular activities out over the school days not stacked up all on one.

Travel Tip

Extroverts enjoy interaction with others — allow them to be involved in many group activities.

Now what about the extreme extroverts? Back to the analogy of hours in a day: If the extrovert is awake 14 hours in a day he or she would want stimulation 12 to 14 of those hours. Metaphorically, the extrovert's brain is a sleepy brain and craves stimulus to keep it awake. For this reason, they need external stimulus for their brains to be happy. Remember, being an extrovert does not necessarily mean a person is outspoken. My son Colton leans toward the extroverted side, but you would never describe him as outspoken.

Being an extrovert does not necessarily mean that the individual likes to get his/her stimulation only from people. Some prefer to interact with machines, computers or nature. Since it is relatively easy to gain desired stimulation from other humans, however, many extroverts gravitate toward other people. You may find them going to a busy mall on a weekend just so they can be in a high-stimulus environment. They will attend every socially exciting event possible. For this reason, others may label them as "party animals." Unlike introverts, this group tends to be impulsive and welcome risk.[5] High-risk activities provide extra stimulus and keep their brains happy. Extroverts seek exciting activities and situations that would overwhelm introverts. In fact, studies have shown that their performance will actually improve with external stimulus or distractions.

This group wants to be involved in everything. Generally they are very competitive because competition increases the level of stimulation. You might find them picking arguments or debating over insignificant things — not to cause problems but to obtain additional stimulation. Their craving for stimulation can put them at higher risk for "getting in trouble" as their brain's search for ways to avoid boredom.

So what do you "pack" for your extroverts? A large variety of material that will allow you to constantly change things up. Be sure that you take a lot of highly stimulating "detours" on your journey. Such "detours" include busy field trips, extracurricular activities, books, computer programs or learning games that will keep their attention. Avoid having them focus on the same subject for too long. It may mean that you only spend 15 to 20 minutes on one topic. Even if you don't complete it you can do something else then come back to it later. This way their brains are more likely to remain interested. Switch it up a little. Be creative. I think you will be happy with the results.

[5] This could also point to another brain personality connection that has to do with what we call "brain lead." I will briefly discuss this in chapter seven.

Above all, be sure you validate the individual brain of each child. Avoid using a cookie-cutter approach with all of your kids, which is a mistake common to many public schools. You want to teach each one at their own speed and with their own unique learning style in mind. Understand the amount of stimulus each one needs. In short, what you "pack" for each child will be different. If you find yourself doing the same thing with each one, take a step back. Reevaluate what you may have missed. Ask for their input then show appreciation for their ideas and implement them as much as you can. The more comfortable and fun we make the learning experience the more our children will retain.

It's time now for you to take another break. Think about yourself and your family. How do you fit into the information we just discussed? What sensory or learning preferences are present in your family? How introverted, ambiverted, or extroverted are you, your partner, children or friends ? Think about how valuable this information can be to improving the communication within your family relationships. Your effectiveness as your children's teacher will also be greatly improved.

Wait! We are not finished "packing" yet. We have one more thing to take into consideration. I know your "suitcases" are bursting; however, you will need to adjust some of your supplies based on one last thing — and this is: Am I packing things in a pink or blue suitcase? Yes, I am going to discuss gender. We all know that male and female brains are definitely different. How we communicate — and yes even teach — varies based on whether we teach a boy or a girl. You will continue your "packing" with this in mind in the next chapter.

Chapter Four

Boy Stuff, Girl Stuff: The Reason the Supplies Are Different

There's a strong relationship between differences we see in the brain and the way children act.

RUBEN GUR, PHD, DIRECTOR OF THE BRAIN BEHAVIOR LABORATORY AT THE UNIVERSITY OF PENNSYLVANIA, IN PHILADELPHIA.

In considering your "packing supplies," you need to consider whether you need a "blue suitcase" or a "pink" one. You may think this topic strange for a book on homeschooling; however, we all know that physical and hormonal difference exist between men and women — and the same applies for the brains of boys and girls. These differences affect the way that each sex learns and matures. As I emphasized in the previous chapter, I will be discussing several differences, but what does "different" mean? Not superior or inferior — just different. Different is not a competition of who is better at what — just an explanation of why boys process information differently than girls. I also want to remind you of the 100-percent rule. You will rarely find that 100 percent of the traits apply 100 percent of the time. Most of the time, you will likely find that about 70 percent of the characteristics apply the majority of the time. Again, don't over analyze it.

The Changes Started Before We Even Thought About Taking This Trip

Let me start at the beginning. No, I am not talking about birth. I'm talking before that event. You see the difference in the male and female brain begins before birth. Early in pregnancy, if the Y chromosome is present, the male brain receives a chemical bath. This alters several things and, oddly enough, adds a slightly pinkish color to the brain. This bath will alter the size of 12 different areas in the brain. Nine of these areas will be larger in the male brain. From a schooling point of view, the most interesting change involves slowing the maturation of the left side of the male brain. In other words, at birth, the right hemisphere is more developed in the male brain.

In most brains[6], the left hemisphere is primarily responsible for spelling, reading and certain math skills. Three of the 12 areas that have been identified as different are larger in the female brain. One of these involves a zone in the left hemisphere related to language. This area is 11-percent denser with neurons in the brains of females. When you put this together with the fact that the left side of the brain is more developed in little girls, is it any wonder that in general they learn to speak, read and tend to get better test scores earlier in language and reading comprehension than little boys? You will also find it interesting that girls typically use both sides of the cerebrum for processing language, and they may have the potential for multiple speech centers in the brain.

Travel Tip

Use more patience when teaching your little boy speech, reading or spelling.

On the other hand, boys typically have one primary speech center and they tend to only use the left side of the cerebrum when processing

[6] R. Carter, "Mapping The Mind," Phoenix, London, 2004.

language. The structural difference requires more patience when teaching little boys speech, reading and spelling. In general and especially during kindergarten and primary grades, it would not be as easy for boys to use the left sides of their brains, as it may not be as developed as girls' brains in the same age range.

We also find some very interesting statistics[7] connected to learning disabilities and gender. For example, males have a higher rate of speech problems, up to five-times higher. One out of every 2.6 boys between the ages of 3 to 17 will also have speech problems. This ratio is not as high in girls. The rate of mental retardation and autism is also higher among boys than in girls. In review of reading problems, you will find that one out of every 10 little girls struggle with reading. The figures[8] with boys show a difference. Nine out of 10 boys age 3 to 17 have reading problems and show higher rates of dyslexia. Some of this could be because the left brain does not mature as fast.

If you take this factor into consideration, you might ask, "Are we confusing speech and reading *problems* with simply *learning* these skills slower?" Do boys develop these problems because they are expected to perform at the same level as little girls with the same level of instruction? One might consider cause and effect of our expectations on learning for little girls versus boys. Might boys have easier time learning if you approached it with a different teaching methodology and gave them more time when the subject involves speech, reading, spelling and language? You should definitely think about it.

Whatever the results could be, when you teach boys you may find that more attention needs to be given in the area of reading and speech. If you know this information upfront, you can adjust your teaching accordingly. It is unfair to expect young boys to perform in these areas at the same level as girls.

[7] Summary Of Health Statistics for U.S. Children; National Health Interview Survey, 2000, and National Center for Health Statistics, Vital Health Statistics 10(213).
[8] National Health Interview Survey.

Remember, we're discussing differences. I'm not implying one gender is superior to the other.

I had an experience relating to this topic with Colton, my youngest boy. When he was around age 9, I had him take an extracurricular six-week creative writing class. It sounded fun, and he was interested in it so he took it. Big mistake! Not that the class was a mistake, but the instructor. She had this wonderful resume' of experience in teaching on this topic, but obviously knew nothing about the brain and learning. After a couple of classes, she pulled me aside and expressed her concerns that Colton was far behind in reading and writing. While I cannot remember the exact dialog, the gist of the conversation was that she felt I should put Colton in a remedial class. After taking a deep breath so that I didn't lose my composure, I calmly yet firmly explained that I was fully aware of brain development and learning. I informed her of how the left side of the boys' brain develops slower and that he would catch up over time. There was no need to be concerned.

Needless to say, Colton did not want to stay in that class and I did not want to subject him to any negative thought or words that may have resulted if he had stayed. Just for the record, Colton is now quite an accomplished reader and has given presentations involving reading in front of hundreds of people. I wish that teacher could see him now. Lesson learned — each brain develops at different rates. Avoid assuming that because your child's skills don't measure up to traditional ideas that he or she suffers from a learning disability.

While the boys have the challenge of a slower-maturing left hemisphere, the girls have the opposite challenge. At birth, the left hemisphere

Travel Tip

Exercise patience with little girls when it comes to activities that involve spatial visualization.

is more developed in the female brain. This gives the female an advantage in kindergarten and primary grades (compared to little boys), as so much of the typical curricula is involved with the left hemisphere. It also means that girls may not use some right brain functions as easily as boys. Skills like spatial visualization. Therefore, girls may not do as well with subjects that require this skill. Try to avoid expecting girls to have as good right-brain strengths as boys in the early school years. Boys may dominate right-brain skills for a while.

Travel Tip

Women are likely to have a global processing style while men seem to think laterally.

Another interesting area of difference in the brains of boys and girls involves the corpus callosum, the largest of three bridges that connects the two cerebral hemispheres. The corpus callosum in girls tends to be larger. This is because more connecting fibers go from the right hemisphere to the left hemisphere in female brains. These fibers may also be larger in diameter. This could be why women appear to balance many different things at once while men seem to be more single-thought focused. I have heard it compared to the difference between a narrow two-lane country road (e.g., male brain) versus a major city freeway (female brain). Women can just jump from the right to left hemisphere with greater ease because they have more "roads" to do so. This results in women having a more global thinking style while men think much more laterally. It also means that it takes more energy second for second to run the female brain because, with its global thinking style, if any part of it is on, all of it is on.

You will find this apparent in children as well. Little boys may tend to focus on one thing at a time. Boys may be more intent on one project or subject while the girl talks and works on a project all at once. Avoid assuming the female's apparent multi-tasking ability is an advantage though — it exhausts the brain more. Research[9] shows that the brain of the male is more energy-efficient than that of the female. All of that bouncing back and forth from the right side of the brain to the left can use up a lot of energy.

Talk, Talk, Talk

Who uses more words per day? Males or females? Studies on this subject vary, but the information is amusing to review. In general, males tend to use more words at work and far fewer words at home. Estimates are that females speak from 20,000 to 50,000[10] words per day. Yes, you read that right, 20,000 to 50,000! In comparison, boys or men generally speak about 2,000 to 12,000 or words per day — a big difference! The type of words used is also quite different. Females tend to use more descriptive words like adverbs and adjectives that result in longer sentences, while males tend to use nouns and verbs and shorter sentences. These differences may be partly structural and partly learned behaviors. Regardless, this information can help you communicate more effectively with children.

 Travel Trivia

Women speak from 20,000 to 50,000 words per day versus men who speak 2,000 to 12,000 a day.

Girls will likely use a lot of words to express the answers to your questions or to state what they feel. When girls problem solve, they may talk it out or say the process out loud. On the other hand, boys may have a more difficult time putting their thoughts into words. Their answers will be shorter and more specific. They may not talk the problem through but rather process silently and internally and communicate only the answer. They may not want to state how they

[9] "Sex Differences In The Human Corpus Callosum: Myth Or Reality?" From The Neuroscience And Behavioral Reviews, Volume 21(5), 1997.
[10] Arlene Taylor, MS PhD www.realizationsinc.org, "Why Men Don't Listen And Women Can't Read Maps" by Barbara and Allen Pease, "Brain Sex" by Anne Moir and David Jessel.

"feel" but only what they "think." It may even be hard for boys to explain how they came up with that answer. So it may take more insight on your part to decipher your boys' needs.

IQ tests of adults yield pretty interesting information as well. As I will discuss later in the book, I am not a fan of tests — especially in children; however, since we have the information we might as well put it to good use. Men do considerably better on tests measuring spatial skills. Seventy-five percent of men place higher than women. They also score higher in mathematical reasoning. On the other hand, Women score higher on verbal tests and areas of language fluency. Their scores are also more evenly distributed across the subjects tested; however, men tend to have more highs and lows and score really well on specific subjects and not so well on others. As you teach, you will see this reflected in your children.

I would be remiss if I didn't share this next brain fact with you — even though it is not directly connected to homeschooling — I do feel as a parent it is good information to know. It has to do with the hypothalamus, a small part of the brain located in the upper-brain stem. The hypothalamus plays a key role in regulating body temperature, hunger, thirst, sexual activity and more. It is interesting that this portion of the brain is larger in most men than in women. Another portion of the brain, the hypothalamus nucleus also relates to sexual and social behavior — and it's larger in most men. The neuroscience world hotly debates this difference. Some researchers think[11] that this brain difference explains why men tend to be more sexual than women — or for the sake of parenting why boys tend to be more sexual than girls. I think either way that practical application of this information enables better understanding of the opposite sex — and makes it worth paying attention. As children hit that wonderful time in life known as puberty, knowledge of this brain difference can be especially beneficial.

[11] "Nature Neuroscience," March 7, 2004.Allen Pease, "Brain Sex" by Anne Moir and David Jessel.

Preparing Children for Life's Journey

I thought this chapter would be a good place to discuss some societal views of the different sexes. When you homeschool you have the advantage of helping your children develop a healthier sense of self. Not that every parent — whether they homeschool or not — can't accomplish this goal. When you homeschool your kids, you have the advantage of more quality time spent with your children. You also enjoy minimized negative input often given in public schools.

Even though society has made significant forward movement to establish equality between the sexes, there is still a long way to go. Statistics[12] can be fascinating to review. Here are a few things to ponder. Men with high IQ scores are usually high achievers in business; but for women there is little relationship between high IQ scores and business success. The money distribution isn't equal either. Women are generally still paid less to do the same job as men — about .75 cents on the dollar.

You may find it interesting that men generally have a more comfortable view of their own sex. Some studies suggest up to 75 percent of women said that at one time or another they wished that they could have been born male — or at least had access to the same opportunities or privileges as men. Yet males usually say that they would not want to be a female. Only 1 in 100 said that they would like to be a woman. Some men even say that they would not want to change places with a woman for even a day. In my opinion, more effort needs to go into helping both sexes appreciate their own unique gifts and qualities.

The media also plays a role in how we view the sexes. Magazines and advertisements aimed at women tend to deal with interpersonal relationships,

[12] United States Department of Labor Women's Bureau Statistics and Data.

understanding oneself, how to succeed on the job, tips for homemaking and parenting, and how to look more attractive. While magazines and advertisements marketed to males emphasize action, performance in areas of sex, sports and business, and how to make and or repair items and gadgets. One study[13] analyzed one hundred children's books. It showed that the books contained twice as many boys as girls and seven times as many men as women. Storybook sons outnumbered daughters more than two to one — not a lot of positive imaging for our little girls

Girls aren't the only ones that receive negative programming. Society often fails to validate the need for touch as much for boys as we do girls. Some studies have shown that mothers touched their female children more than their male children after they were over six months of age. Fathers also touched their daughters more than they do their sons. In the previous chapter, I talked about the importance of touch for optimal physical and emotional health. You may want to pay extra attention to the physical reassurance that you give to your male children.

As you consider the proceeding information, think about what message it sends to your children, whether boys or girls. Room for improvement exists. It may be difficult even for a forward-thinking person to fight deeply in-grained societal expectations when it comes to gender. However, any extra effort you exert will hopefully help the next generation improve in attaining gender equality.

Blue Suitcase? Pink Suitcase? What Do I Pack?

Now that I have discussed several differences between boys' brains and girls' brains, you can appreciate that you need to "pack" differently for each — or should I say *learn* how to deal differently with each. Avoid expecting the same

[13] "Differentiation Of Gender Roles And Frequency In Childrens Literature" by Leslie Dawn Helleis.

progress out of your little boy that you do out of your little girl. *Never compare the two.* It would be like comparing an apple to an orange — both are healthy and nutritious, but definitely look and taste different!

At parts of your journey you may have to slow the car down a little for your sons. Come up with ways to tie in the brain's creative right side since it is stronger in little boys. Maybe label things in your house to help them read. Incorporate a lot of songs to teach spelling, rhyming and reading. (The center for native music ability in the brain is on the right side). As they age, it may take until their preteens or early teen years before their left brain talents fully develop. Be patient.

Your little girls on the trip may not need very much extra "packing." They have the left brain strengths that give them a leg up in the early years. A great thing about homeschooling allows you to go as fast or as slow on a subject as you need. You don't have to worry too much about cramming things in to get it finished by a certain deadline or finding extra things for them to do if they get bored. You can (within reason) move at their pace with their individual brains in mind.

Travel Tip

Blue Suitcases
✓ Use labels to help boys read
✓ Incorporate songs to teach spelling

Pink Suitcases
✓ Modulate your teaching — fast or slow — to go at your girl's pace

Okay, now you know what to "pack" and what color "suitcase" to use for your individual child's brain. Let's move onto the "itinerary." What will your school schedule be? What will work best for your family? I will discuss this in some detail in the next chapter.

Chapter Five

You're All Packed! Now the Itinerary: Make a Schedule

> ❝ *The key is not to prioritize what's on your schedule, but to schedule your priorities.* ❞
>
> STEPHEN R. COVEY

So what will be your "itinerary" or schedule? You have choices. Will you do a year-round or fall-to-spring school year? Will you have the same vacation days as the public schools or will you make up your own? These options are important to consider. Your brains are used to traditional public school structure and schedules. When the "back-to-school" sales come around, you probably go shopping. You plan your vacations and family trips in connection with the school calendar. You may even want your school day to begin at the same time the public school day begins. The problem is that you may find yourselves subconsciously following something that doesn't work for your family.

Yearly Schedules versus Nine Months or Year-Round

School calendars vary from district to district, county to county, state to state, and of course, country to country. You will find supporting arguments for each available calendar-year option. Consider several factors when deciding what schedule works for your family. Remember, you are now homeschooling. You don't have to follow the norm or go with the status quo. Choose what fits your family — a point I continue to emphasize throughout the book. No two families are alike. Each one has different needs and circumstances. Make it an imperative to find out what works best for everyone in your family.

Some families prefer the annual school-year calendar; but most of us realize that our children don't stop learning in June after the "last day" of school. Sure children may not be following a textbook but their brains are still taking in information. Why not continue with academics? Proponents, such as Sam Pepper and Dr. Charles Ballinger of the National Association for Year-Round Education, think it's easier on the child's brain for them to continue steadily learning. Some believe that students receive a more consistent education with this type of calendar. A study conducted by the California State Department of Education showed that standardized test scores in reading improved by more than 13 percent. While I have no faith in standardized testing, this may impress some who do.

Another line of reasoning supports the year-round calendar. Some think review time required at the beginning of the nine-month calendar wastes time. Some teachers say that it takes too long to bring students up to speed. I wonder whether students have a hard time getting back into the swing or the teachers. Either way, I know many home-schooling families that prefer year-round school. So if you find year-round school works best for your family then go for it.

Other people prefer more of a fall-to-spring-type school year. This schedule gives your family a summer break — several weeks when you don't have to think about school. You will also find a number of studies[14] that support this option. Some education experts, such as Wes Walker, Dr. Leo Wisenbender,

[14] You can find these studies at www.geocities.com/weswalker99/#articles, "Public Schools Early Start Is Another Calendar Fad" in the Florida Times Union of August 8, 2001, and a British Columbia Teacher's Federation study conducted in May, 1995: "Do Year Round Schools Improve Student Learning?"

Travel Tip

My boys enjoyed 2.5 months when they didn't have to worry about school work.

and Christopher Newland, PHD, suggest a year-round calendar has negative effects on student morale. They also cite studies and tests to support their hypothesis. Lawsuits have even been filed against different districts because they changed to year-round school. Oh that's good, waste precious tax dollars in the courts. A bunch of adults bickering over how year-round school affects students. They will probably decide that they need to add yet another test to the list so that they can evaluate the effects. Did they ever think of asking the students what they think? Sometimes adults can learn a lot from a child's perspective.

I chose a traditional nine-month calendar because my boys had friends that were in public school — and they wanted to have time off in conjunction with their friends. We did however vary the days off throughout the year. When I planned our family vacations it was never connected to the school calendar. (In the next chapter, I will discuss more on how we can teach and learn regardless of location.) At times, they needed to work a little extra on some subjects over the summer, so we paid some attention to these areas. For the most part, the boys enjoyed knowing that they would have two and a half months when they didn't have to worry about school. I just want to emphasize this worked for our family and may not work for you. Evaluate your circumstances, discuss it with your family, and make the choice that best fits everyone.

Wake up! Let's Start The Day! What Time Do You Begin?

Take a look at the typical day for a family that utilizes the public school system. Most get up early morning, say, 7:00 a.m. Get ready for school, eat a quick breakfast, get dressed (although with what kids wear to school these days you would never know it), walk or be driven to school or the bus, (if they have to ride the bus they may have to get up even earlier), and arrive at school and start classes. Next, they spend 45 minutes on each subject (whether they need 15 minutes or an hour to learn it well). Then, hopefully, they will eat a quick lunch, and go back to 45-minute classes. While in class, they anxiously await the final bell, collect their homework books, pile them into their backpacks, walk, ride the bus or get picked up, and go home. Once home, they eat a quick snack, pull out their books, and do a couple hours of homework. Once finished, they now have a small amount of family or play time. Get ready for bed, go to bed, and wake up after not nearly enough sleep and repeat. *Where is the fun in all that?*

Don't get me wrong, I am not saying that you should run your life "footloose and fancy free" all of the time. Life where there is no accountability for deadlines, appointments, and commitments. I am saying what works for some doesn't work for all. The typical public school schedule could be really hard to keep for an adult — let alone a child. A child's mind forms partially through play and imagination. This growth becomes somewhat interrupted when they spend most of their time in school and focused on homework. Childhood should be fun. In my frank opinion — and this is just that … my opinion — far more emphasis gets placed on academics and not enough on our children's much-needed emotional support and growth.

Travel Trivia

Children between ages 5-9 need between 10-11 hours of sleep each night. Children between ages 10-12 need over nine hours of sleep.

When thinking about this subject try not to forget to factor in sleep. The rigid public school schedule doesn't take sleep into account. Experts like March Weissbluth, MD and Richard

Ferber, MD, say that children ages 5-9 require between 10 to 11 hours of sleep each night. Are elementary kids really getting this much? Children between ages 10-12 need a little over nine hours of sleep per night. At this age, kids grow and change and require a lot of sleep, which makes it very important. During the adolescent years, sleep requirements range from eight to nine and one-half hours. Keep in mind that these assertions are generalizations. Each individual may vary, especially depending on their level of physical activity and personal health. The bottom line is most people are sleep-deprived. This includes a lot of children. Be sure to consider sleep when you set up your family's school schedule. The sleep-deprived brain is not going to understand and learn things as well as the one that gets adequate rest.

You should also note that young brains take time to become fully alert. This transition seems to be especially true for teenagers. It may have to do with how much emotional growth takes place during this stage in their lives. Whatever the reason, I suggest you start the school day later in the morning to enable a kid's brain to be more receptive to learning.

You will also want a flexible schedule so you can allow for a lot of extracurricular activities. Our brains learn so much better through experience. Over the last few decades, public schools have been hit hard with budget cuts. This situation has forced public schools to cut a lot of programs that add variety to learning. Field trips and creative studies — like music, shop and art — have suffered. If you have a flexible schedule throughout the school year you can be more creative with your time. Flexibility allows you to participate in as many extra learning opportunities as you can.

Now what worked for us? I am going to let you in on a secret. One of my favorite things in life is, sleep. I love sleep. After a long day of work the best time of day for me is bedtime. I found that the same held true with my boys. So we rarely started our school day before 9:30 a.m. Not that we would sleep un-

Travel Secret

I love sleep and so do my boys.

til 9:00 a.m., but we just weren't in any hurry to get started. We took our time to wake up, eat breakfast, and leisurely start the day. Yes I said "leisurely." Remember, keep the brain comfortable and it is more receptive to learning. Put it under stress and learning will be less effective.

We also never scheduled a certain amount of time to be spent on each subject. How long we spent was not nearly as important as how much they learned. Each child had their own strengths and weaknesses in different subjects. Sometimes they would "get it" in 15 minutes and we would move on. Other times we might have had to spend a couple of 30-minute sessions on the same subject for them to understand the concept. I say a couple of 30-minute sessions because research[15] shows that the brains ability to retain information starts to decline after 45 minutes without a change. So splitting the time up allowed their brains to rest. Then we would return later when the boys and I had a fresh look on the subject.

This approach worked for us. Each family will have different circumstances they will need to consider. Just try not to allow societal expectations to dictate how you will run your homeschool. Take the time to communicate with your family and figure out what works best for you. In the long run, you will all be happier, which is your overall goal.

Okay, you have chosen your "map," "packed" the necessary items with the brain in mind (no pun intended), and made up your "itinerary." It looks like you are ready to go. The next chapter will take a look at the options you have in setting up and running your day-to-day school.

---

[15] "The Change Up" in lectures by Joan Middendorf and Alan Kalish, Indiana University.

Chapter Six

Load Up! Let's Go! Get Started!

> *Earth and sky, woods and fields, lakes and rivers, the mountain and the sea, are excellent schoolmasters, and teach some of us more than we can ever learn from books.*
>
> JOHN LUBBOCK

Okay, by this point you should know what color "suitcase" you will use. I have hopefully helped you figure out what "provisions" to pack for each of your children. Now let's move on to loading the car and getting started. This chapter will be much easier to cover — not a lot of technical details to consider. My main goal is to get you to begin to think "outside of the house." No that's not a typo, I did mean "house." I am going to start by having you visualize a trip — and think if you have ever found yourself in this situation.

You are a passenger traveling by car to some distant location. The driver is one of those people focused on getting to the destination. They have no desire to stop and see the sites. They just want to get from start to finish as fast as they can. On the other hand, you prefer to enjoy the ride. You know … take your time and see what there is to see along the way. Perhaps even

Travel Alert

Don't forget to stop at the historical landmarks and vistas.

take an extra day or two; however, the driver has other plans. Now as you drive along you see a sign for a vista point or a historical landmark. You might make the passing comment, "Gee, it would be nice to stop and see that." The driver responds, "We'll see." Unfortunately, you approach the exit and realize the driver isn't slowing down. In fact, they whiz past the off ramp and continue, leaving the beautiful vista behind.

When you ask, "I thought we were going to stop?" They reply, "Oh yeah, that's right. Well it's too late now, maybe next time." Perhaps the situation is even worse. Maybe the person's focus means they completely ignore your need to stop and use the facilities. As your bladder fills up, you realize the clueless driver doesn't understand the situation has become imperative. It takes you jumping up and down in the front seat and banging on the dashboard to make them realize your dire need to stop. Sound familiar?

This reminds me of the road trip my family took when I was little. It was our first trip to Disneyland. I was maybe six or seven years old. I remember driving during the night to get there. When I woke up, we were in the parking lot of Disneyland! It must have been early because there were almost no other cars around. I was so excited! I had wanted to go to Disneyland all of my life. (Yeah, that is a long time when you are only seven.) I recall anxiously waiting to get in, holding my tickets, excitement running through my body. Then finally the park opened! We walked inside the gates, and I was too excited even to stand still. My sisters and I just couldn't believe it. We're in Disneyland! What did my father do? He stopped and got a park map and schedule of all the shows for the day. Then he proceeded to take *forever* — well, it was probably more like 30 minutes — to map out where we were going to first, second and so on.

You can imagine our frustration. As small children, the last thing in the world that we wanted was to follow a map. We just wanted to go ride the rides. We wanted to see Mickey, Minnie and Winnie the Pooh. We didn't care about sitting and seeing the Golden Horseshoe Review. On the other hand, my father was concerned with reaching his goal of doing things in a structured, organized way. How exasperated we were! It truly affected how much we enjoyed that day.

 **Travel Alert**

Please make your homeschooling "trip" as memorable as possible, so you never look back with regret.

You may be thinking, what's the point? You are about to take a journey with your family. My goal is to help you make this trip as enjoyable as possible for everyone involved. Your homeschooling time — once complete — should be a time you fondly remember and never look back on with regrets. If you aren't careful, you sometimes create the same problems that I described in the above story. You can be so focused on the goal of educating your children that you forget to stop and have fun. You may think, "Okay, I'm going to homeschool my children, but to make sure that I do it right, I will structure things exactly the same as the public school system." If you are not careful, this can diminish the joy of the experience. Let me explain.

You probably went to traditional public school with a standard classroom. Do you remember the rectangular room with the large chalkboard at one end? The class contained a few rows of desks, lined up nice and straight, and evenly spaced in the room. Along the top of the walls, letters of the alphabet were displayed in cursive and print. It probably had a few windows, some bookshelves, and a teacher's desk in the front. The floor was hard, cold linoleum and the walls were pretty plain.

Travel Alert

Avoid a "collision" with a traditional classroom setting. Your success does not depend on following traditional patterns as in public school.

The traditional classroom setting may be all you know and understand. You may feel that in order to be successful in homeschooling, you need to follow the same basic guidelines and structure. You may fear that if you don't keep things organized and follow the same pattern as in public schools you will fail. You may envision getting your kids up at the same time every day regardless of the circumstances. Having them eat their breakfast, change their clothes, then sit down at their desks, and dutifully do their schoolwork. In my opinion, application of the traditional model is a huge mistake. Keep in mind that one of the benefits of schooling your children at home is to have flexibility in *all* areas, from the curriculum that you choose to the way you set up your classroom. Now try to open your mind to some different ideas and see if they don't help make this trip more enjoyable.

Travel Tip

Location doesn't matter for classroom setup. Focus on what needs to be done, not so much on how it gets done.

The Setup

In our home, classroom setup was very flexible. When I schooled my boys there was an area of the house that you could call a "center for school-related items." For us it was a portion of our back porch. We had their desks set up in this area. I also put up commonly referenced and colorful maps and posters. The area contained shelves and drawers that held school supplies, pencil sharpener, etc. However, my kids rarely sat at those desks. We relied on the area more for storage of school books, pencils, papers and all of their necessary school equipment.

On most days, you could find my sons doing their school work in the dining or living rooms. Whenever we did our reading together, it was almost always on one of the couches. If they were reading to themselves, they may have been on the couch or maybe in their rooms lying on their beds. Sometimes they were outside, sitting on a deck chair or out in the wonderful spring sunshine. At times, they would even wander down to the barn to read. Location was not important. What mattered was we allowed the boys to be comfortable and happy. This non-traditional concept may be a hard to accept at first, but open your mind and think outside the usual parameters. Focus on what *needs* to be done, not necessarily *how* it gets done.

While I allowed the boys to do their schoolwork pretty much wherever they wanted, I did have a couple of exceptions. One was when they were writing in workbooks or when they were practicing handwriting. While doing this activity, they would have to sit at a level area so they could write things down legibly. If they were using the computer, they were sitting at the computer desk. In general though, they were allowed flexibility to do their schoolwork wherever they were comfortable. In this way, it maximized the brain's ability to retain information. This teaching method also keeps the brain's needs in mind; but what else does the brain like? I'll tell you....

What Does The Brain Like? Fresh Air
Okay, so I emphasized physical comfort in terms of body position and location. Comfort can also be affected by the environment. The brain learns better when the right conditions exist in the environment. Fresh air is important.

The Federal Clean Air Counsel and NASA conducted studies on indoor air quality. They found that during the winter months, especially if you have a house that is closed up, air quality can become poor. You may want to consider air filters or even better, plants. Yes, large-leafed plants. These same studies showed that plants such as philodendrons can improve the quality of the air. One study found that placing plants in the classroom raised student productivity by 10 percent. So try to have one plant for every 100 square feet of your home. You will be healthier and again, your brain will be happier.

If you can, try to keep the air temperature semi regulated as well. Think of it this way. It is not good when the brain is distracted. If your body is uncomfortable for any reason, let's say a pebble in your shoe, a too-tight belt, or if you feel too hot or too cold your brain cannot focus on learning. It will pay attention to your body not to the lesson at hand.

What Else Does The Brain Like? Movement

Travel Trivia

Standing up increases blood flow to the brain by 15-20 percent.

A lot of physical movement also benefits and optimizes learning. Just getting up and moving around increases blood circulation to the brain. The more blood movement to the brain the more oxygen it receives. The brain requires a lot of oxygen compared to the rest of the body. It only accounts for two percent of your body weight but requires 20 percent or more of the oxygen. Studies[16] on the brain and movement show that standing up increases blood flow to the brain by 15-20 percent. So encourage position changes and frequent movement during the school day.

[16] "How The Brain Learns Best" DVD by Arlene Taylor

When children are young they are often encouraged to be active. As they get older, however, this tends to change. Adults tell them, "Be Still. "Sit down and focus." A study[17] on movement, the brain, and adolescents, showed that 50 percent of them needed "extensive mobility," 25 percent needed "occasional movement," and the remaining 25 percent needed at least "minimal movement." So, age does not change the brain's need for physical movement.[18] Be careful to avoid making an adolescent's brains unhappy. It may rebel and refuse to learn like we want it to. No, I don't think any of us parents want an unruly rebellious teenage brain around.

Anything Else The Brain Likes? Yes, Water and Natural Light

Things like water and natural light or full-spectrum light can also make the brain more comfortable and facilitate improved learning. Most people still don't appreciate the value of good clean water and lots of it. Not only does it help to rid the body of toxins but in addition it helps keep blood freely moving. This is critical for transporting sufficient oxygen and glucose to the brain especially during heavy study time. Take advantage of the comfort of schooling at home and make sure that your children drink plenty of water throughout the day. Remember too that our brain likes things that are natural. Allow your kids to work close to a window that provides natural light. Maybe you live in a part of the country that has a lot of low light days during the winter. If this is the case, try installing some full spectrum lights. It will benefit not just the student's brain but the brains of the entire family.

Research on full spectrum lights and depression has shown some fascinating results. Some people suffer from a condition called Seasonal Affective Disorder (SAD).

Individuals that battle SAD have symptoms of depression during the low natural light season of late fall and winter. Doctors find that use of full

---

[17] "How The Brain Learns Best" DVD by Arlene Taylor
[18] Movement is especially necessary for the ADHD child's brain to learn.
See http://www.physorg.com/news162554898.html

spectrum light during dark months improves SAD's symptoms by supplementing natural light.

This information helps us to appreciate that everything in the environment affects our brains — even light.

The Brain Likes To Sing. Music

Music is another fun and important thing to add to your child's curriculum. The brain really likes music. The brain has an area primarily responsible for music awareness; but the whole brain benefits from learning and listening to it. A lot of research has been conducted on music and the brain. Some researchers think that the earlier in life you can expose your children to music the more intelligent they will become. Some studies, such as Colwell 1994 and Taniguchi 1991, suggest certain types of classical music enhance learning. A lot of debates go on over this topic as well. What type of music is best, how soon should children be exposed and at what decibel level should it be delivered?

Whatever the different opinions may be, it cannot be argued that music does activate the brain. If someone learns to read music and play a musical instrument the brain likes it even more. It really doesn't matter what type of instrument you learn. Learning how to *read* music primarily involves and exercises the left hemisphere of the brain. Learning to *play* an instrument involves and exercises even more of the brain. Musicians that play complex stringed instruments have more connections in the section of the motor cortex connected to finger movement. (Sorry, I know that I said this chapter wouldn't have a lot of technical stuff in it.)

In short, reading and playing music offer a healthy workout for the brain. Even if you don't have extensive musical training, there are several areas of the brain that light up when music plays. So it may enhance learning if a certain type of music plays softly in the background while you children do their school work. If anything it will at least get their brain's circulation going.[19]

Think Outside the House

The brain also likes variety. It learns better when you constantly "switch it up." Open up your way of thinking and realize that your children don't have to read from a textbook to learn. As a matter of fact, you may find that they remember things better when their brains can make multiple sensory connections. In previous chapters, I discussed brains with different learning styles; but keep in mind that even though most people have one preferred learning sense their brains do take in information from all of the senses — the more creative activities that involve all of the sensory systems that you can incorporate in your daily schooling the better.

Travel Tip

Do fun things like cooking to teach your kids math. Have your child make a big cookie and teach him or her measurements or division.

You can really apply this well when studying math. Most math books are very basic. A page covered with words and equations. The majority of the books that I have seen have very little or no color, which is boring for the brain. However, I think that it is one of the easiest subjects to be creative with. When teaching basic adding and subtracting skills you can use all sorts of tools. Make good use of any tangible objects to make studying math fun. Jelly beans were one of my favorites, but the selection can be limitless. Coins, Legos™, building blocks, coffee beans, popcorn and the list goes on. How fun is it to tell your child, "We are going to do math now, go outside and find 20 little rocks." Do you think they will have more

[19] "Music with the Brain in Mind" By Eric Jensen

fun with this than if you sit them at a desk with a book?

One way that my youngest son enjoyed doing math was by cooking. When you teach things like multiplication and division, cooking is a great way to go. Have your child make a really big cookie or pie. The process of making it teaches them measurements. Once they finish, ask them to divide it among family members. Then ask them to think what they would need to do if you had a big get together or family reunion. They have to figure out how many of these big cookies they would need to make if each person only gets 1/4 or 1/8 of cookie. This is a great way to teach the basic multiplication, division and fractions with a little chemistry thrown in.

When you move onto more advanced math, say algebra, just make your creativity more advanced. Get out of the house. Give them a tape measure, pad and pencil. Have them measure an area of your property and figure out the perimeter. Ask them to call the local lawn and garden store to find out how much a roll of fencing costs and how many feet are in each roll. They can then calculate how much fence they need, how many rolls of fencing it will take to fence the area, how many fence posts it will require if you place one every six feet and so on. Take it one step further and ask them to figure out how much grass seed you would need if you seeded the area they just measured. Then they can calculate the cost for seeding. Go yet another step further by having them put it all together and find out what the cost per square foot is in the entire project.

Now if you are thinking, "I live in a little tract home or an apartment I don't have anything to measure." Open your mind, think creatively. Go to the park and mark off an area for them to work with. It doesn't have to be real. You can expand this with a multitude of other potential projects. Have them repeat the earlier process, but this time make the area round. Ask them to figure out how much paint you need and what the cost per foot would be to paint the outside of the house. Create different scenarios. Build a deck, carpet the inside of the house, design a pool having them calculate the volume, the options are limitless. In the process of doing all these imaginary projects, you have not only taught them algebra but also the practical application of it. More importantly you made it fun! It is the active process of using all the sensory systems that is important.

 Travel Tip

Teach kids math through practical daily living exercises. Give them a budget and send them shopping at the grocery store.

Another great way to teach practical math is to give your child a shopping list and a budget. Actually take them to the store and have them purchase the items. Make it challenging. Only give them enough money to barely make the purchases. Tell them to pay attention to the prices. If they can buy everything on the list they can keep the change. Do this several weeks in a row, taking them to the different grocery stores in town. It won't take them long to learn the practical math and the value of money and keeping a budget. Avoid thinking that this can only be done with teens. Young ones can learn a lot from this lesson. The earlier they learn to appreciate the value of the dollar the better.

You can be creative like this with all of the subjects. For example, when you teach the alphabet get out a pan, put some flour in it and have your child draw the ABC's in it. You can also have them finger paint the ABC's while they sing the ABC song. Another fun interactive thing to do involves making dough out of flour and water. Have them make the letters of their name or the alphabet and bake them. Better yet, use sugar cookie dough for this activity — and they can eat the finished product.

When I was teaching the boys how to read and spell, I put labels all over the house. The doors, couches, pillows, things in the kitchen, there were PostIt® notes all over the place. It may have looked a little strange but it made it a more memorable way of learning. The more associations you can make for the brain the better. If your children's brains can connect one fact that they learn to 10 memories, it will recall the information more completely than if it only makes a couple of connections.

Travel Tip

The world is your classroom. Get out and teach your children by using the natural environment.

The classroom also doesn't have to be inside. It is wherever you want it to be. The whole world can be your classroom. For example, subjects like earth science create ideal opportunities to go out and learn. Our children will never learn as much from a book as they will from seeing and feeling what really happens in the environment. Have them make a compost pile outside, take them on a nature hike and turn over a dead tree, collect water samples from the stream, take it home, and look at it under a microscope. Go outside on a night when moon is dark and study the constellations. Repeat this every month and watch how their positions change in the sky. Do you think this will stick in their minds better then reading it from a book? Of course it will!

Field trips are another excellent source for learning. I tried to incorporate them as often as possible and still don't think that I did enough. For example, when we were studying alternate forms of energy we drove through Altamont Pass in California to watch the windmills, went out to the Monterey, California to watch the power of the waves, and took a tour of a hydroelectric dam in Folsom, California.

When we were studying the Gold Rush times we went to several historical sites and toured gold mines. The boys interviewed an old hard rock gold miner. It was so fun to watch them ask him some questions then listen intently as he would give the answer. I could see the wheels in their heads turning as they were visualizing what he was saying. They were thinking about what it must have been like taking the mining car deep into the earth. How dark it must have been. What would happen if the mine caved in? What must the wives of these men have felt at the sound of the warning bells? History becomes so much more real if kids can stand in the spot where something exciting from the past actually happened or touch ruins left over from an ancient civilization. Include field trips in your homeschooling. It will be so much more memorable for your children.

Creative writing for some children can be a challenge. They may find it uninteresting. Again, try to do something that doesn't require standard workbooks and ideas. Two of my children, Alex and Colton, were never really that crazy about this subject. This meant that I had to come up with some creative ways to incorporate things that were of interest to them.

So when my boys were young I had them produce a newsletter. It was called, "The Little Mountain Press." They each had to write an article on whatever interested them. Alex, my oldest often wrote something about an idea he had for alternative transportation or new form of energy. Kasey, my second son, always liked writing things about his animals or some pygmy goat show he had attended. (He raised pygmy goats.) Colton my youngest was the resident chef. He was constantly coming up with creative ways to cook a quesadilla. They would also interview a senior from the community and put the interview on the "Life and Times" page. They were proud to have a group of friends and family to distribute the newsletter to. This activity was a fun way to get creative writing worked into the curriculum. They hardly realized it was school work.

Make Good Use of Computers

Travel Alert

The computer allows children to virtually travel the world.

When the weather is bad or you don't have the resources to travel, computers can be another great tool. Many of the programs available now are interactive, which is good because it involves movement, touch, sight and sound. Math and spelling are fun when made into games. Some available geography programs like National Geographic, Sheppard Software, or Where in the World is Carmen Sandiego? allow your kids to travel the world. They are able to see sights they may never see in person, but the digital photography in these programs provide a not-so-bad substitute. Plus, they can solve a mystery and chase down a criminal at the same time.

As I mentioned in Chapter 2, we used a really fun high school life science program.[20] It was very interactive. You started by walking into a building and up to a receptionist. Then you could choose to go into the library and read a book that was full of visually appealing pictures. They might go into the science lab and do an experiment or dissect a frog. Yes, you could dissect a frog on the computer. A word of caution, this is such a tech-driven society that it is easy to get caught up, albeit unwittingly, in using the computer too much. Make sure that it supplements all of the other creative and outdoor learning that you do. Try not to allow the computer to replace it.

In the end, I am trying to help you see the classroom becomes whatever you make it be. Make schoolwork whatever you want it to be too. Use your creativity. Try to incorporate practical reasons for learning things. Get your kids up, move around, engage all of the senses, and explore the world. Your

[20] Glencoe McGraw-Hill High School Life Science.

kids' memorable lessons may not happen in a classroom or be read in a book. These lessons may be those creative, unique and fun "experiences." Remember, the most awesome classroom ever is the world.

Chapter Seven

Making the Grade: Why The Climb Is Too Steep For Some

> *I think the big mistake in schools is trying to teach children anything, and by using fear as the basic motivation. Fear of getting failing grades, fear of not staying with your class, etc. Interest can produce learning on a scale compared to fear as a nuclear explosion to a firecracker.*
>
> STANLEY KUBRICK, LEGENDARY DIRECTOR

What is a grade anyway? Is it some letter between "A" and "F" that somehow represents your intellectual level? By the way, have you ever wondered what happened to letter "E?" Did people who made up the grading system deliberately leave it out? Or did they just forget the alphabet? It makes you think, doesn't it?

Okay, so maybe I have a few issues with the public-school grading system and even sometimes in homeschooling. Traditional grades fail to show a fair evaluation of the student's abilities or intellect. Consider the emotional impact on a student or child condemned or criticized for not receiving an "A" or "B." What if they can't score these grades? What if it is in a subject they will never use again? What if it doesn't interest them? What if their brains find it too hard? You may think differently, but let me explain a little more about the brain. I want you to pull the "car" over at the "brain vista point" and take a good look at it.

Let's do an exercise to help you to understand this better. Clasp your hands in front of you. Now look at them. Which thumb is on top? The right or left? If the right thumb is on top you are right-thumb dominate. If the left is on top you are left-thumb dominate. Now, change your hand position. Make yourself put the opposite thumb on top. How does it feel? Is it as comfortable as the first position? Now let's do the same exercise with our arms. Fold your arms the way you would naturally. Which arm is on top? If your left is on top you are left-arm dominate. If your right arm is on top you are right-arm dominate. Now change the position again. Put the opposite arm on top. How does it feel? Is it as comfortable as the first position?[21]

You can consciously go around your automatic innate lead, but it takes more brain energy. These exercises help to reinforce that people tend to have leads throughout their entire bodies — lead eye, lead ear, lead hand, lead leg and so on. So too with our brain.

The information that I have been sharing in this book on the brain comes from a variety of studies and research modalities. For example, the new brain scanning technology has allowed experts in the field of brain function to peer through a window that has never before been opened. They can now actually watch the brain as it thinks. They can measure the amount of glucose burned each second as a person performs some cognitive task. What is revealed is beyond fascinating. By looking at the results of PET[22] scans, experts believe that most brains have an energy advantage in one of four natural

[21] This is not the same as "handedness" or right handed or left handed.
[22] Positron Emission Technology

divisions in the cerebrum (or the brain's thinking portion). Researchers such as Benzinger/Sohn believe that most people are born with this biochemical predisposition. This information's impact is huge — especially when discussing the topic of grades.

This data explains why there are things that just come easily for some people, but can be incredibly difficult for others. We have all had those moments when we feel a little jealous of something someone does with ease — some things we can never get right no matter how hard we try. When this happens we may say with a sigh, "They are just *gifted* at that," or, "It comes so *naturally* to them." Arlene Taylor, my friend and mentor, calls this their "innate giftedness." While you can become good or competent in certain tasks due to practice, what I want to highlight are those natural gifts.

What makes you naturally good at certain things? *Your* brain! Research shows that your brain requires less energy to do the things that you're naturally good at doing. Up to 1/100's the amount of energy. There is a decreased resistance across the synaptic gap in the area known as your brain lead, or as I like to refer to it, your "home." In an earlier chapter, I referred to brain lead and said that I would briefly discuss this topic. Now, I want to give you a general idea of the different brain leads and their implications for homeschooling and education. However, as I stated before, remember the "100-Percent Rule." Not everything will apply to everyone all of the time. Also, try not to forget that as we discuss the different brain leads please remember they are simply different, not superior or inferior, just different.

The Left Brain Leads

The left brain — whether front or back portion — is the less emotional side. It has considerably less neural connectors to the portion of the brain called the limbic system, which is the area connected to emotion.

Travel Tip

The Basal Left Brain Lead

✓ Enjoys organizing

✓ Likes performing detailed, repetitive tasks as long as it understands the reason for the tasks

When you process functions — such as fact based decision making, delegation of authority, ability to set and pursue goals — the front left portion of the brain activates. How does this play out in human behavior? A take-charge person good at directing others in a logical manner likely has a "home" that resides in the frontal left part of the brain.

What portion of the brain do you typically use when you do sequential organizing like spelling, making lists, performing detailed repetitive tasks, tracking time and money, or recalling facts? Primarily the basal left does this type of work. Children and adults at "home" in this area of the brain will naturally be gifted in these tasks. This means they may only spend up to 1/100ths the amount of energy in this area of the brain.

The Right Brain Leads

The right side of the brain, front and back has more connectors to the emotion section of the brain, the limbic system. This is why those with right brain leads tend to display more emotion. When you do things like harmonizing, you use mostly the basal right portion of the brain. If you are recalling the emotion connected to a memory, you use this portion, as well. The center for native music ability is believed to be housed

Travel Tip

Frontal Right Brain Leads

✓ Enjoys daydreaming

✓ Gifted at brainstorming or non-fact-based problem solving

in this section. So people with this brain lead generally have a natural musical gift. Drama connects strongly to this quadrant too. Therefore, people at "home" in the basal right are typically dramatic.

Now if you use the frontal right portion of the brain, you may be doing activities like daydreaming, brainstorming visualizing (internal mental picturing), thinking outside the box, or non-fact-based problem solving. When we visualize and think outside of the box we are probably using the brain's frontal right portion. If "home" for you is in one of these two portions, you may be gifted in some of these functions. Remember, it will be easier since you burn less energy in that area.

An important note to understand: If your "home," or for the subject of this book your child's "home," is in the front left portion of the brain then the most *difficult* area of the brain for you to use is the basal right. It is farthest away from your "home." If you have to "drive" down there, so to speak, you burn the largest amount of fuel. Why? Neural connections run vertically and horizontally — not diagonally. The same rule applies for all of the leads. Bottom line: the most energy-intensive area for any brain lead is the one directly to the diagonal.

 Travel Tip

Frontal Left Brain Lead

✓ Likes to take "control"

✓ Gifted at fact-based decision making

✓ A "likes-to-take-charge-type" person

Do You Get It?

Did that make sense or are you totally confused? Hopefully as I continue, the clouds will begin to lift and your view of the brain will become clearer. Let's apply these ideas to children and school subjects. Frontal left children will likely do well in subjects like algebra, calculus or mechanics. These school-related functions primarily involve this part of the brain; however, these children may find it difficult to emotionally harmonize things or partake in drama or music. Why? Because these abilities are in the diagonally opposite part of the brain. So for children "to travel" all the way down to that region will take a lot more energy. It would be like a child having to hike up a hill with a heavy backpack on his or her back to get to their destination.

While growing up, I was close to someone who often drove me crazy. She never had any problem directing all of us children or telling us what to do. In retrospect, I now realize she was and probably still is a frontal left brain lead. At the time, we used to think that she was so bossy. Now that I have a clearer understanding of the brain, I can redefine her actions and eliminate negative words and say, "She liked to be in charge. That's okay. It was just one of her gifts." So you may have that little child always taking control of other children — one that tells everyone what to do and how to do it. In this case, the child's "home" more than likely resides in the frontal left portion of the brain.

In general, basic school subjects like spelling, reading or basic math, use the basal left portion of the brain. In school, children with this as their "home" will usually do very well in those subjects. These skills will likely come easier since they don't have to use as much energy as the other children. However, they may have a hard time with trouble-shooting and visualization skills that use the frontal right portion of the brain. These abilities reside in the diagonally opposite part of the brain, which is too far away from "home." It takes too much energy to get there.

Travel Tip

Basal Right Brain Lead

✓ People Pleasers

✓ Excels in music, cooking, drama, foreign language or art

✓ May have trouble making decisions

Children at home in the basal-right portion of the brain will likely be our little people pleasers. They may feel deeply for living things, people and animals. They may do well in subjects like music, cooking, drama, foreign languages and art. They are typically gifted at anything that requires emotional display or connection with people; but it may be hard for them to make decisions or tell people what to do. Why, because to use that part of the brain they have to "travel" farthest away from "home." It will take a lot of energy.

Children at home in the frontal right potion of the brain may be good in school subjects that require thinking outside of the box, visualization and creative problem solving. They will probably be constantly creating new things. They might come up with the most imaginative and abstract ideas — sometimes ideas that seem a little strange to most but to the frontal right children they can fully visualize them and it makes perfect sense. Be sure not to discard those ideas though. Some seemingly outlandish ideas from people in the past gave us things like air flight, the internal combustion engine, and so on. This group of children often has to work hard on basic school subjects that require spelling and reading because that is the diagonally opposite side of the brain and farthest away from "home." They will have to use a lot more energy to "travel" all the way down to the basal left part of the brain to access those sequential fact-based memories. So, how is all of this connected to grades?

What about the Grades?

Oh yeah, that's right I started this chapter discussing the grading system so I will get back to that subject. I know this may be confusing, but now put all of the pieces of the brain together and you will start to see how it applies to children and learning. Let me give you a couple of examples. Perhaps you have an introverted, frontal right, kinesthetic little girl. How will she perform in the subject of spelling? Remember, she has a harder time accessing that part of the brain. Her introverted brain may also have a difficult time with too much stimulus if put under pressure. Then add that for a kinesthetic, reading the spelling words and definitions is not in line with her learning style. So in the end, it requires a lot of extra brain energy for her to get a "B" or "C" in this subject. She may work really hard and still not achieve 100-percent accuracy. It may just be too difficult for her brain.

Now imagine that you have a seven- or eight-year-old little boy who is at "home" in the basal right part of the brain. Let's say that he has a visual learning style. He may try so hard to audibly sound out those words in his reading book. He wants mommy and daddy to be happy with him. So he sits for long lengths of time trying and trying. In the end, however, he still struggles to read even the simplest words. You may begin to think that he is dyslexic or has a learning disability. Wait! Remember, he is a boy. The left side of the brain isn't quite ready to read well yet. Think of how devastated he may feel when he thinks he let his parents down because he only gets a "C" in reading. When in truth he deserves the biggest "A" you can give him because he worked harder than all of the other children just to get that "C."

Is the view becoming clearer now? Are you starting to see the details in the errors that can happen when too much emphasis is put on a letter grade over on a letter over hard work? Granted, most children will at one time or another, for whatever reason, not put enough effort into their school subjects. At this point, you as homeschooling parents may need to come up with a creative way to motivate your kids to try a little harder. Keep in mind, you will help them develop much more confidence and a better level of self-esteem if you praise them for their strengths rather than shame them for their weaknesses.

Tests, Tests, and More Tests. Is This Truly a Necessary Part of the Journey?

Travel Trivia

Traditional education doesn't account for "brain lead" when giving tests.

Wait for just a minute I have something that I need to get, hold on, where is it; oh there it is under my desk. What is it? My soapbox! Let me get on it for just a few minutes. Tests are one of my pet peeves. When you add up all of the information that I have discussed so far I think you can understand. When you consider that grades are not a true evaluation of a child's intellect, how can tests be? Yet they are so important in the academic world. Schools advance children or hold them back based on test results. Universities or colleges accept or reject teens based on these results. Think about the word "rejected" or the term "held back." Does either of those make you feel good? Of course not!

I just explained to you how hard it can be for a child to get good grades in a subject that uses portions of the brain far away from their "home." Traditional education does not account for brain lead when giving tests. They don't give tests based on your brains "home's" location. They don't factor in introversion or extroversion level. They test all children in the same grade together without thought of gender.

You also have a couple of "brain-year" gaps in children of the same age. Just because two children are the same chronological age does not mean that they are equally as mature. Some experts think that the gap could be as much as two year's variance in both directions. In other words, you can have three eight year old children. One can be very mature for his or her age, maybe acting more like he or she is 10. One may act his or her age. The third child may act like a six-year-old. Yet when it comes to testing, traditional education measures them all against the same bar.

Consider also that when the brain senses stress, emotional or physical, its protective part kicks into high gear. In order to power the extra work, it now thinks it needs to do, it steals as much of oxygen as it can from the thinking portion of the brain. This explains why when you sometimes take a test you just can't think of the answer. You get frustrated because you know that you have the answer stored in your brain somewhere but you just can't access it. Then after you finish the test, you may walk out of the room and the answer suddenly pops into your brain. Once the stress of the test is over, the action part of the brain allows the thinking part to have its oxygen back and you can find the answer.

When you consider all of the contributing factors, introversion/extroversion level, gender, learning preference, brain lead, age variance, and lack of oxygen supply in a stressed brain, can you understand why I think the way that I do? You may remember that when I homeschooled my boys I used a charter school as my map. In order to benefit from the funding that they provided, there was a trade off … tests. If your children were enrolled in the school you had to agree to have them take the STAR tests each year. While I obviously didn't like it, I complied. Each time that I dropped the boys off for the tests, I would tell them the following, "Remember, it is only a piece of paper with silly little bubbles on it. It is not a reflection of you as a person or of how smart you are. Do your best and don't worry about the results." In short, I think strongly that parents should never allow themselves to rate their children based on test results. If you are not careful you can set your kids up for self-esteem problems without even realizing it.

Alright, I will get off my soap box and put it back under my desk for now. Forgive me if I have offended you — that is certainly not my goal. I want to assure you that I am not saying that we shouldn't encourage our children to do their personal best. That is the key though; it should be *their personal best*.

Not what scholastic experts, teachers or superintendents of schools consider best. Not what the average best is for that age group; but rather what each individual child's best can be, with the whole brain taken into consideration.

What Is The Answer?

Travel Tip

Keep your child's beautiful brain in mind when assessing their levels by how well they do their daily work.

If you can't use the grading system or don't care about test results, how are you to understand your children's skill levels? When I schooled my boys I did my best to keep their beautiful brains in mind. I would assess their levels by how well they did on their daily work. If they would get most of the problems or questions on their work pages correct, I knew that they were getting it. If most of them were not correct, I knew that they needed more work. Instead of saying "test time" and sitting them down with a pen and paper to take a "test," I would conduct more of an oral evaluation. I would ask questions and then have them explain the answers. I found this to be a more effective way to evaluate how they were doing scholastically without emotional repercussions of a grading system or tests.

Please remember to make the best choice for you and your family. It may be that you think differently than I do — and that's okay. Our wonderfully different opinions and personalities add beauty to the world. If your perspective differs from mine, make it work for you. Just try to keep the brain in mind. If you do that, I have no doubt that it will make for some easy "downhill glides" and fewer "uphill climbs" in this wonderful journey you and your family are on.

Chapter Eight

Can School Make My Child Ill?
The "Sickening" Truth

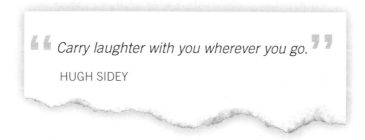

" " *Carry laughter with you wherever you go.* **" "**

HUGH SIDEY

Have you ever planned a fun and exciting trip — a trip that involves the whole family? Maybe it was a road trip, a few days at an amusement park, or perhaps a cruise with a whole itinerary of shore excursions? You spent months planning every detail — especially if you are a basal left-brain lead. Then the time came to leave. You packed your bags with everything you needed — and you were off. At first, everything went great. Then all of a sudden you or one of your family members got sick. Your plans to see the sights, lie on the beach, or take your tours were ruined. You wanted nothing more than to go home; but what about all of the money you invested? All of the plans you made? You were looking forward to this trip for so long. Not only were you or your family member miserable, but then you had to cut your trip short.

While you may have never experienced this exact scenario, I think you probably have something that comes close. How is this experience connected to school and an environment that can make your child sick? I already discussed the benefit of homeschooling to avoid exposure to many germs. In this chapter I want to enlighten you about something else that may cause physical illness, which is something that, if you aren't careful, can happen within your home — an experience that may cut short your homeschooling journey.

When I went to college I took classes on natural health. One of the courses I took was on the subject of "psychoneuroimmunology." Yes, that is a word. It is the study of the connection between your emotions and your immune system. If you get the chance, I suggest reading a book titled *Head First* by Norman Cousins. In his book, Cousins relates what life experiences lead him to deeply investigate this field. He then shares some of the studies and the work that has been done related to the topic. It is a good book to gain an understanding of the brain-emotion connection without too many technical details.

This research reveals how much our emotions — positive or negative — can alter our immune system's effectiveness. The portion of the brain that houses the immune system is called the limbic system. Interestingly, the limbic system also is in charge of our emotions. An undeniable connection exists between the two. If you feel down emotionally then your immune system will be down. If you feel up emotionally your immune system will follow. Studies show a change in the natural disease killer t-cell activity happens with encouragement of positive emotions. The opposite is also true. Negative emotions can negatively affect production of these same cells. Now, I don't want you to think that I believe all ailments can be prevented or caused by our emotional state; however, compelling evidence suggests a definite connection — one that

Travel Alert

Feeling down means your immune system will be down. Feeling up means your immune system will be up.

Travel Tip

"We awaken in others the same attitude of mind we hold toward them."   AUTHOR UNKNOWN

should make us pay attention to our negative emotions and more importantly, those we might trigger in another person. As parents we should be especially attentive to the impact on our children, which is the point of this chapter.

The years your children's brains develop and learn are so crucial. Things people say to them and impressions made may shape their thinking and self perception for life. Now if you educate them at home, you have the opportunity to foster extra positive input. In this book, I have tried to encourage you to teach with the brain in mind. If you don't, it may lead to unnecessary frustration and possibly a negative emotional tone. A negative emotional tone can lead to a suppressed immune system. A suppressed immune system can, in turn, lead to susceptibility to sickness and chronic disease.

Travel Tip

Watch what you say to your children — it can affect them both emotionally AND physically.

For example, if you don't teach with your child's learning styles in mind, it may lead to frustration — negative emotion. If you expect your little boys to achieve the same grade expectations as your little girls, it may lead to your little boys feeling something is wrong with them — negative emotions. If you think that all of your children should be able to do well and excel in every subject, it may lead to disappointment for you and your children — again, unnecessary negative emotions. Now, factor in reports on the connection between the negative emotions and your health. Could you possibly set your children up for potential health problems in the future? It is definitely worth seriously considering.

Positive Reinforcement

Travel Tip

Fill your lives with laughter and make your school days fun.

While discussing the topic of emotions, I should consider positive reinforcement. Positive reinforcement leads to positive emotions. I am not saying that you should praise your children over every little thing and take it to an extreme. I am saying that direction can come from a negative, reward-punishment angle. Wisdom suggests you handle this approach with caution. You need to make sure that you use validation versus negative statements.

Sometimes you may inadvertently put your children on the failure path, because you set unrealistic expectations on their brains. Try to appreciate the strengths and non-strengths of each individual. Work hard to validate the uniqueness of each child's mind and personality. Be perceptive of why they do things the way they do. Be understanding of why they may have difficulty in a subject rather than thinking something is wrong with them. Help them to know that some things will come easy while others things will be difficult — but that's okay. They are who they are.

Laughter

Laughter is good medicine — this is something we've all heard. Laughter affects the brain and, in turn, the immune system. Do a search on Google and type in "laughter is good medicine." You will probably have over 500,000 site links pop up. Read a few of them. I am sure you will find the information very enlightening. Laughter would be a fun thing that you can add to your daily routine. Fill your lives with laughter whenever you can. Why not incorporate humorous books into your reading curriculum?

A few years ago, I found a desk calendar at the book store that had a funny office prank for each day. They were just silly nonsense things that you could do every day to break the monotony and make everyone laugh. Why not incorporate something like this in your school day? Of course, if you did something silly each day, that could lead to your children thinking you are a little strange. Too late for me, my kids figured out that I was a little "out there" a long time ago.

If you put a little extra effort into making your school days fun, I know that you will be happier with the results. Try to keep positive, up-building thoughts and words a part of your daily routine. When you do this, you will literally be happier and healthier, studies prove it. However, no matter how hard you try, you will likely hit a "bump" or two in the road. Maybe even have a "blow out," a "breakdown" or run into a "road block." If this happens on your home-schooling journey what will you do? In the next chapter I will discuss some of the challenges you may encounter along the way.

Chapter Nine

Blowouts, Breakdowns and Roadblocks! What to Watch For and How to Maneuver Around Them

> **"** *An obstacle is often an unrecognized opportunity.* **"**
> AUTHOR UNKNOWN

No matter how well prepared you are for any trip, sometimes things just go wrong. We all know of someone who had a vehicle break down or had a flat tire on the road. Sometimes they can be easily fixed; sometimes they are close calls; and sometimes they cause major delays.

A few years ago, my sons and some friends took a trip to an area in Nevada called "Sand Mountain." Its name describes it exactly — a huge mountain of sand where people go to ride all different types of off-road vehicles. On the way there, they got a flat tire on the truck. They pulled over, took the compressor out of the trailer, and started to refill the tire. As my oldest son and his friend were doing this activity, they noticed a bubble start to rise up in the tire. Realizing the impending danger, they quickly jumped back just in time as the tire literally blew up. Fortunately, no one was hurt. They replaced the tire and continued their trip.

Your homeschooling journey can also at times be challenging. There may be a few "flat tires," "breakdowns," or "blowouts." You may hit a "roadblock" and you don't know how to maneuver around it. When this happens — and it more than likely will — don't panic. If you know ahead of time what some of the challenges may be, you will understand how to handle them. Over the next few pages, I will cover several of the common issues you may encounter. If these happen along your journey, try my suggestions and see if they help.

Getting Their School Work Done

Travel Tip

If you find you're on the "right road," but your child struggles to get his or her work done, go for more positive reinforcement or ideas to motivate.

Probably one of the most common problems involves getting your children to do their work. This situation may happen because your child loses motivation. In this case, think about how you are teaching. Could it be that you stopped doing things with the brain in mind? Review the previous chapters on learning styles, gender and brain lead. See if perhaps you took a wrong turn somewhere and started subconsciously back down the traditional route. If you find this to be true, pull out your "brain compass" and make the necessary adjustments. See if this helps.

If you find that you are on the right "road," maybe go for more positive reinforcement or ideas to motivate your kids. Consider tips like setting aside time to incorporate one of those aforementioned field trips. Maybe it's time for an even bigger break — a vacation that has an educational purpose (however in my opinion, you can find educational value in any vacation). The answer may be even simpler than time out to travel. There were days when I just needed to remind my boys that the sooner they finished their work, the sooner they could do something else. I hope one of these suggestions helps get your kids going again.

Boredom

Another problem — boredom — may arise and require the creativity that I talked about earlier in the book. It may be that you find yourself in a routine of just doing school work. It might be time to "mix it up." Take a different approach to the subjects. Maybe look into using different books that interest your child more. Get some catalogs or go to a book store and look at the selection they have. Ask for your child's input. Let them help you choose books that are more appealing to their brains.

If you have only one child being schooled at home, you may need to increase their interaction with other children. As I mentioned in chapter two this could also be a challenge for families that have chosen the "Complete Independence" map as well. If this is the case try the following. Check out your local library. You can make good use of their reading hours. You can enroll your child in a gymnastics class or look into local community theater or arts program that he or she can get involved in. Check to see if any homeschooling groups meet in your area. If there are none maybe you could start one. You never know, it could be other parents would also enjoy the support. By breaking up the days or weeks with activities, you can often solve the boredom problem.

I Don't Understand This!

What if your child just doesn't get a particular subject? First, think about "brain lead." Is this a difficult subject for him or her because it is not his or her "brain home?" Please realize it may take a while — and be patient. Try some creativity. Think about how to explain the subject with your child's brain lead in mind. The problem may not be with your child — but rather be a subject too far from your own "brain home." Perhaps it takes you too much energy to explain it. If it is something that you can't quite get, how can you explain it to your children? Now may be a good time to ask for help.

When it came time to cover algebra with my kids I hit a "pothole." I had a hard time explaining some of the more complicated processes. I could do the problems myself and come up with the correct answer, but to explain how I came up with the answers didn't work for me. So I found a math tutor. He met with my boys one day a week for a semester or two — and that's all it took. The boys whizzed through the book, and we saved a lot of frustration. Tutoring may be a resource that you want to access. If you have a hard time finding anyone local, you can find tutors online as well. Try out this resource. You might find that it is just the right fix.

Isolation

Feelings of isolation can also be an issue for some families. These feelings can be especially apparent if your chosen "map" calls for complete independence. You will find that some of the suggestions for resolving the problem of boredom can apply here as well. Get involved in local community projects that include other families. This way your children can get to know other children in the community. Take initiative and set up times for the kids to get together and have fun. If the other children go to traditional school so what? It only means that you will have to work around their schedules.

Travel Alert

Overcome Isolation

✓ Join homeschooling support groups

✓ Set up field trips

✓ Use the Internet

✓ Tap into online support groups

Connect with the closest homeschooling support group. See if they have activities for you to get involved in. Set up field trips or meetings at locations that will be an equal travel distance for you and other homeschooling families. These social activities make great opportunities to meet and exchange thoughts, ideas and encouragement. It may mean that you have to do most of the arranging, but I think you will be pleased with your new connections. Remember to use the Internet. If you can't find local activities, connect with online homeschooling support groups. Do a Web search to see if your state has a homeschooling coalition or association. They may have events you can attend. You will quickly realize the homeschooling community is huge. You just need to tap into it.

Socialization

Okay, this is another one of my little pet peeves. Almost every time I talk to a skeptic of homeschooling this is the first thing that they bring up. What do they think I do? Do they picture me locking my children in the house, never allowing them to be seen by the outside world? How strange do they think I am?

For the record, I do think this is the easiest problem to overcome. Just because our children aren't socializing at school doesn't mean that they aren't socializing. Plus, who says that all of the association in public schools is *good* association. Anyway, if you feel that this is a concern for you, here are some suggestions.

Enroll your kids in extracurricular activities. My kids were always enrolled in some form of extracurricular activity. One year it was rock-climbing classes. Another year it was gymnastics and a computer class. They have taken art, music and archery. They spent eight years in 4-H™. Needless to say, they had plenty of socialization. You can take advantage of any classes offered in your community. Simply find out what is of interest to your child then get them involved.

Promote community volunteerism. Be sure not to discount the value of having your kids associate with community members. Many volunteer opportunities exist where they can help their elders. Have your kids help them do

Travel Tip

"Keep away from people who try to belittle your ambition. Small people always do that, but really great people make you feel that you, too, can become great."
MARK TWAIN

simple projects around their homes. Spend time at senior centers to help out. For the most part, those in advanced years enjoy being with young ones. They can share the wisdom of their life experience, and your children can benefit from what they have to say. I feel this is a win-win situation — and the problem of socialization is solved!

Form fun groups or associations. Younger children can be well served by play groups. Older children will enjoy more structured activities. You can schedule weekly, bi-weekly or monthly activities with other kids in the community. You can even keep it as simple as inviting them over to play together in your backyard.

Your kids can form a study group with other homeschoolers in your area. Invite other kids to participate in study-group activities and teach them the value of teamwork. They can work on a fun indoor or outdoor project. Maybe they can do something like plant a garden, or do a fun science experiment — it doesn't matter as long as they learn to work together.

What to Say to the Critics

Over the years, homeschooling has become more common. I have seen many

Travel Alert

When the critics attack NEVER take it personally.

change — both good and bad. Back before I started my journey, I was watching a popular talk show host interview a homeschooling family whose children had gone on to Ivy League colleges. What the family had to share was wonderful, but the way the audience treated them ... wow! Here the "proof was in the pudding" so to speak as evidenced by their children's accomplishments. Yet some of the audience comments were unkind. Now more than 15 years later, you would think that with the increased popularity in homeschooling, you would not have to deal with criticism. Well, you thought wrong.

Many critics feel that all children should be schooled in the traditional school system. They may say things like, "What qualifications do you have?" or "Your kids need to be in a regular school or they won't grow up normal." or "How will they get into college?" You will find a variety of objections. The key: Don't take it personally. When you meet people who doubt your ability to do a good job, don't let them shake you. Remember, no one is more qualified to care for your children then you. As parents you are natural teachers. Who taught your children to talk? You. Who taught them to button their shirts? You. Who taught them to tie their shoes? You. The list goes on and on and on. Homeschooling takes your teaching to the next level. According to the last Census, 1.1 million children were homeschooled in the United States. If the parents of 1.1 million children can do it, so can you. According to widely-repeated estimates, as many as two million American children are schooled at home, with the number growing as much as 15 to 20 percent per year.[23]

Travel Alert

Support System Check List

✓ Ask a family member to give you a day off

✓ Remember to give your marriage attention

✓ Take time for date night

✓ Take a weekend break with your spouse

✓ Leave the house for a mini vacation

✓ Remember to relax and "refuel"

[23] U.S. Census Bureau "Home Schooling in the United States: Trends and Characteristics" by Kurt J. Bauman

Running Out Of Gas

Homeschooling parents spend every day with their children. In addition to daily care they add "teacher" to their resumes. You will be responsible for making up creative lesson plans, setting up field trips, arranging extracurricular activities, and evaluating your children's schoolwork, etc. It won't matter your level of organization or ability to schedule, you will have days when you are ready to stop the car, jump out, and run around like a crazy person. It is normally on these days (in my experience) you may feel a lot friction between you and your children. Friction that if allowed to build can lead to a "tragic crash" in your homeschooling "car." You want to avoid this if at all possible. So before you buy yourself, or your children straitjackets, learn to pay attention to the warning signals.

Most new vehicles today have warning lights that come on when your tank gets too low on fuel. When that happens, you don't have far to travel before you have to "fill 'er up." Homeschooling is no different. When the low fuel warning light goes on in your brain, you need to pay attention. If you neglect to do this, you may find yourself stuck on the side of the homeschooling "road," empty and wasted, ready to quit.

To avoid hitting total burnout, call on your support system. You will find that you probably have more friends and family that you can rely on then you realize. In the beginning, this was difficult for me to accept. If you haven't figured it out yet, I am pretty independent. It was not always easy for me to admit that I needed help, but when I did, I found that the assistance my family gave me was invaluable.

My sister, Tara was awesome. She would often spend a day with the kids, helping them with their schoolwork so I could take care of my other responsibilities. Other family members also pitched in. My mother-in-law would take the boys every now and again just so I could get some much-needed down time.

This was a half-day or full day when my focus was not on the lesson plan or the schoolwork, but on relaxation and refueling. Without these much-needed breaks, it would have taken some of the enjoyment away from our journey.

My boys even benefitted from these breaks too. They may have still been required to do their school work, but I was a lot less grouchy after my breaks. I would have a refreshed feeling and a more positive attitude. Refueling is a good thing, so remember to tank up!

Time for an Oil Change

Now I am not a marriage counselor, but I have been successfully married for almost 24 years. When you decide to homeschool you generally do it as a family. However, I have noticed that it seems to be, for most families, the wife has the more active role. Sometimes this can become a source of friction between husband and wife. Not because Dad isn't supportive of the arrangement, but because he may just need Mom's time too.

So for the ladies reading this book, try to remember that your men also need your attention. When this issue became apparent to me, my husband Paul and I started planning time alone away from the boys. It can be as simple as a dinner and a movie, a quiet drive in the car, or a lunch date. Then every two or three months, go away for the weekend — just the two of you. It doesn't have to be an expensive trip. It can be dinner out or a night in a hotel that's right in your own town.

One time, Paul and I stayed in a historic hotel not more than 15 miles from our house. The next day we slept in, took our time to check out, ate breakfast, walked through some shops, saw a movie, and then returned home. On other occasions, we would go camping for the weekend just the two of us. Whatever your favorite couples outing is, I suggest you take time to do it whenever you can. I'm recommending you avoid losing your marital identity. Remember, you aren't just a mom and teacher, or father and teacher. You are also a wife or husband and for the two of you to have long-term success in your marriage, remember your spouse needs you too.

Did I Miss Anything?

Several more "potholes" or "blowouts" may come your way while on your journey, and each family has their own unique challenges. You may face something that I didn't have to deal with and have not thought about. Perhaps you aren't as independent as I am and need more support. Whatever the case, never forget that help is only a mouse click or phone call away. I am sure there are family members that can help and homeschooling support groups abound. You will also find homeschooling coaches[24] to guide you through tough times. Make good use of these resources, fix the "blown-out tire," and get back on the "road."

---

[24] Julie Anderson is also a homeschooling coach. For more information, go to www.quickestwaytoinsanity.com

Chapter Ten

Enjoying Your Road to Insanity!

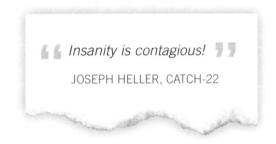

> *Insanity is contagious!*
>
> JOSEPH HELLER, CATCH-22

Wow! We covered a lot of homeschooling ground. Hopefully you gained information that you can use to help make your homeschooling journey a long-term success. If you haven't figured it out yet, I want to help you think about things from a non-traditional view and help you realize that you can think "outside of the house" and do things differently. When you work hard and apply all of this information, the results will be worth it. It will make for a more enjoyable journey — one where you laugh and have fun. The kind of journey the whole family can enjoy.

Another piece of advice on your new "road to happy homeschooling:" Avoid putting a lot of pressure on yourself. Please try not to think that you need to focus every day on creating new ways of doing things or exciting field trips to take. You will have days when you just need to get the schoolwork done. Days filled with textbook studies or required indoor activities — and that's okay. Think back on the suggestions in the book; find the ones that work best for you and your family; and then put them into use and file the rest. Remember, the most important lesson you can take away from this message is: *Always do what is best for your family.* They are what matters most. Just because these things worked great for me, doesn't mean that all of it will work for you.

This subject brings me to the inevitable point that I also must share with you — homeschooling may not work for every child and every family. You may find that one of your children responds well in a homeschooling environment while another child doesn't. You may have a child with special needs and choose to homeschool him or her while you have their siblings in a traditional school. Maybe, you want to have your children be in a traditional school for their K-3 years or all of their elementary grades, but homeschool in junior high or high school. Perhaps it is just the opposite — homeschool in the beginning and then transition into a public school. Again, I emphasize, do what works best for you and your family.

There may be points along your journey when your circumstances change and you need to take a break from schooling your children at home. Sometimes it is your child that needs a break. This happened with my oldest son, Alex. For a brief period of his 3rd-grade year, I was having difficulty getting him to do his school work. This was before I had the knowledge of the brain and learning, so I didn't understand that he was really just bored because the schoolwork was too simple for his brain. Anyway, I had always promised myself and my family that I would stop homeschooling if it caused too much friction. So for a period of about three months, I put Alex in a traditional school. It was a tremendously emotional move, but the results were positive. He realized the wonderful benefits of homeschool — and promptly got back into our homeschool "car."

You too may find that you or one of your children needs to make a change. If that is the case, it would be counterproductive to beat yourself up about it. Avoid thinking that it means you have failed or something is wrong with the way you did things. It just doesn't work for everyone all of the time. You may even have read through the book and decided not to take this journey at all. You may have considered the "map" options and responsibility it will take to make this journey a successful one and decided it is not for you or your kids. If this is the case, so be it. The only people you have to answer to are those you love and care about. They are the most important. Do what is best for those that matter the most.

What Do The Graduates Have To Say?

I thought it would be fun to take a look at the student's point of view. So I asked a few that have graduated from homeschooling over the last several years to give me their thoughts. What did they enjoy or not enjoy? What did they appreciate and take away from their homeschooling experience? Here is what they had to say:

"The thing that I loved about homeschooling was that it allowed me to move at my own pace. I didn't have to spend unnecessary time on subjects that I fully understood. No needless repetition. Once I grasped the concept I was able to move on. In turn, when there where subjects that I didn't completely understand, I was able to focus more time on them. If I had been schooled in a public school I feel that I would have been bored half the time and possibly lost the other half. I believe in homeschooling strong enough that when I have my own children and the time comes to school them I will definitely instruct them at home for at least part if not all of their schooling."

- ALEX ANDERSON

"Homeschooling was a positive experience for me because it allowed me a great deal of flexibility that I don't feel I would have had in a traditional school program. It gave me the ability to choose when and how I did my school work. Due to the pace that I was able to keep in high school, I began my college work before I graduated. This made it possible to complete a third of my degree before I finished high school. By doing this I have been able to reach my career goals earlier in life."

- KASEY ANDERSON

"Homeschool for me was like a roller coaster. It had its ups and downs, twists and turns. At one point, you are having a blast, then the next you are screaming, 'Get me off of here!' However, by the time you get off you really enjoyed the ride. By the way, the whole ride metaphor, was my idea, I didn't get it from my mom. I think she stole it from me, maybe I need to copyright it or something."

- COLTON ANDERSON

"Homeschooling helped me to become more of an independent learner. It also helped me in learning because it provided me more of a one-on-one atmosphere. It allowed me to work at my own speed and level, which helped me to achieve my goal of graduating early. I enjoyed homeschooling very much through my high school years and I would recommend it to anyone!"

- CHELSEA

"Homeschooling was very enjoyable for me because I was able to complete my assigned work more rapidly. By doing this it gave me more time to associate with my friends and pursue my other goals."

- ALEC

"I feel that it is important to go to public school during the early years. That is when you develop social skills and how to deal with people. However, once the kids get older they change, becoming not-so-good associates. Then the schools seem to worry less about teaching and are just trying to keep them under control. For this reason, I was happy to be homeschooled during my high school years."

- RACHEL

"I feel that it was a benefit to be homeschooled during high school. By doing so it allowed me to move through my subjects faster than I would have been able to do in a traditional school. The result is that I graduated early, took the college courses I was interested in earlier, and was able to move on to my life goals."

- ADREAN

Travel Tip

"Whatever you are, be a good one."

ABRAHAM LINCOLN

"Like most kids my age, I started kindergarten in public school at age five. For me it was detrimental. Around the age of seven, I began to have health problems. Then by the time I reached 4th grade I was missing whole school weeks at a time. At that time my mother decided to try and homeschool us (my younger sister and I). While homeschooling I was able to thrive academically. Where I was failing in public school, in homeschool I was now getting A's and B's. Although the damage to my body had been done by this time, at least I was able to learn and progress to the point that by the time I graduated from high school I had a 3.8 GPA.

If I had been made to stay in public school I may never have graduated and who knows how much worse my health would have gotten. Every child is different and has different ways of learning. For me public school was just not the right option, but homeschooling was and it enabled me to grow the same as everyone else. "

- TARA

"I started homeschooling in the 4th grade. It was quite a shock at first, but after some time went by I started to notice I was not being held back as far

Travel Tip

Many children who are homeschooled become self-confident, well-adjusted adults.

as having to stay at the same speed of all the other kids in the classroom. I was able to excel in many of my classes and was even asked if I would like to skip the 5th grade. I continued homeschool all the way through high school and was able to graduate a year early. I was also able to take college courses which helped me to progress as a person and opened a way for new activity in my life. I think it is the way to go for someone who wants to feel somewhat independent and not tied down to a classroom. I loved it!"

- HOLLY

One last quote is from a graduation speech given by a recent homeschool graduate. The "map" or option that his family chose was a charter school. He did his schooling at home but the school had a formal graduation ceremony. I enjoyed his speech and thought you would enjoy part of it also.

"Tonight's graduation is the culmination of our commitment, from the efforts of that first day of kindergarten to now as we await the satisfaction of receiving diplomas ... We all had obstacles we had to overcome ... But we all overcame them and we are here today. Is that the end of our obstacles? NO! We've just begun. There are going to be all kinds of obstacles. How are we going to overcome them? Well I know that when I was at my desk trying to finish up my work, it helped me to think of my goal of graduating. And obviously you all had that as a goal too. That goal that we had set in our mind helped us to just get through whatever work we had to do. So, now as we build our individual lives, we have the joy of setting new goals and accomplishing them. To quote Zig Ziglar, 'I don't care how much power, brilliance or energy you have, if you don't harness it and focus it on a specific target, and hold it there you're never going to accomplish as much as your ability warrants.' So let us focus ourselves on new things."

- CHRISTOPHER

What do you think? I think they are quite impressive. These past graduates all appreciated the benefits of homeschooling even if it was for a few years. Several of them felt that homeschooling gave them a head start on their life without an undue amount of extra work. Each of the individuals I talked to grew up to become self-confident well-adjusted adults or near-adults. In short, the goals of their parents were achieved and the benefit of homeschooling made clear in the success of their children.

Where Do You Go From Here?
So now you've done your research. You've chosen your "map," prepared your list of what to pack and placed it securely in the properly colored "suitcases." You now understand how to teach with the brain in mind and are aware that you have the whole world as your classroom. What next? Start your journey! Be prepared for those uphill climbs. Have your list of the support systems you will call on ready. Make contact with other families taking this same journey and then get going.

In the end, I hope that you have found at least a few if not many gems that you can use in this book. At times, it may have been a little confusing maybe too technical, but I hope you will see the benefit in applying the information whenever you can. Points that will make your journey have fewer "uphill climbs" and be filled with plenty of "downhill slides." You will hopefully have a more enjoyable and memorable trip.

When I look at my boys I see the true benefits of our journey. I have no doubt that homeschooling had a lasting positive influence on them. True there were sacrifices that everyone in our family had to make. My husband had to work long and hard to provide financially for us so that I could stay at home with our boys. The boys themselves had to be understanding and patient with me as I learned to navigate on our trip. Sometimes they had to help me figure out how to get around "road blocks" or change those "blown tires." Yet in the end, it was all worth it. Every "uphill climb" seems like a tiny ant hill when I see what fine young men they have turned out to be.

As I look back over the last 15 years of my life, I can't imagine how it would have been if I hadn't taken this journey. What wonderful views would I not have been able to share with my kids? What exciting moments would I have missed? How much time spent with my children would I have sacrificed if I had sent them to public school? I can't even imagine the answer to those questions. There is no place that I would have rather been then on this trip with my three wonderful children. I hope that you too will be able to look back over your homeschooling journey with the happiness and satisfaction that I enjoy. With memories that you will always cherish and a trip that you will, like me, never ever regret having taken.

Travel Tip

I hope your homeschooling journey will provide you with memories that you will always cherish and a trip that you will never ever regret having taken.

About Julie

Julie Anderson is a 15-year veteran of homeschooling. She and her husband of 23 years have been blessed with three sons. That's right, all boys. If they would have kept going, they could have started their own baseball team! All three of Julie's boys have finished their main academic school years. (Julie says this because she believes we all continue to learn as we go through life.)

Over the years, Julie has learned a few tricks, found some great resources, and met great people that made her homeschooling journey the best trip ever! It is her hope that the tools she provides in her workshops and presentations will help parents to continue and always enjoy their homeschooling journeys as well.

Julie Anderson is no stranger to public speaking. Since her early teens, she has been in front of audiences numbering into the hundreds. During the last 10 years, Julie has been speaking and teaching groups, large and small, on the intricacies of the Brain/Personality connection. She trained under one of California's premier experts on this subject. She has numerous college units in subjects that range from psychoneuroimmunology to deaf studies. She is proud to add to her speaking list, a subject close to her heart, homeschooling.

References and Resources

Realizations, Inc.
Arlene R. Taylor, PhD
www.arlenetaylor.org

"Music with the Brain in Mind"
Eric Jensen

"Brain-Based Learning"
Eric Jensen

"Mind Waves"
Arlene Taylor, W. Eugene Brewer with Michelle Nash

"The Art of Using Your Whole Brain"
I. Katherine Benziger & Anne Sohn

Quickest Way to Insanity…Homeschool Your Kids
www.quickestwaytoinsanity.com

Brain Personality Connection
www.brainpersonalityconnection.com

"Mapping the Mind"
R. Carter
Phoenix, London, 2004

The Alliance for the Separation of School and State
www.schoolandstate.org

Summary of Health Statistics for U.S. Children
National Health Interview Survey, 2000

National Center for Health Statistics
Vital Health Statistics, 10(203)

National Health Interview Survey

"Sex Differences in the Human Corpus Callosum: Myth or Reality?"
The Neuroscience and Behavioral Reviews, Volume 21(5, 1997)

"Why Men Don't Listen and Women Can't Read Maps"
Barbara and Allen Pease

"Brain Sex"
Anne Moir and David Jessel

"Nature Neuroscience"
Allen Pease

United States Department of Labor Women's Bureau Statistics and Data

"Differentiation of Gender Roles and Frequency in Children's Literature"
Leslie Dawn Helleis

"Human Relations Development…A Manual for Educators"
George M. Gazda, Frank R. Asbury, Fred J. Balzer, William C. Childers,
Rosemary E. Phelps, Richard P. Walters

"Public Schools Early Start is Another Calendar Fad"
Florida Times Union
August 8, 2001

Wes Walker
www.geocities.com/weswalker99/#articles

"Do Year Round Schools Improve Student Learning"
British Columbia Teacher's Federation
Study conducted May, 1995

"The Change Up"
Joan Middendorf and Alan Kalish
Indiana University

"How the Brain Learns Best"
DVD by Arlene Taylor

"High School Life Science"
Glencoe McGraw-Hill textbook

National Geographic Software
www.shop.nationalgeographic.com

Sheppard Software
www.sheppardsoftware.com